Greek Style

Greek Style

SUZANNE SLESIN, STAFFORD CLIFF
& DANIEL ROZENSZTROCH
PHOTOGRAPHS BY GILLES DE CHABANEIX

DESIGN BY STAFFORD CLIFF
Art Associate: Ian Hammond

Clarkson N. Potter, Inc./Publishers
Distributed by Crown Publishers, Inc.
New York

TO

JAKE AND LUCIE STEINBERG

HEATHER AND NEVILLE CLIFF

MARIE-JEANNE, JEAN-LOUIS,
AND MARIANNE MÉNARD

ANNE, JEAN-MARIE,
AND LUCAS DE CHABANEIX

Published by Clarkson N. Potter, Inc., 225 Park Avenue South, New York, New York 10003 and represented in Canada by the Canadian MANDA Group CLARKSON N. POTTER, POTTER, and colophon are trademarks of Clarkson N. Potter, Inc.

Manufactured in Japan

Library of Congress Cataloging-in-Publication Data
Slesin, Suzanne.
Greek style.

1. Interior decoration – Greece – History – 20th century.
2. Interior decoration – Greece – Foreign influences. I. Cliff, Stafford. II. Rozensztroch, Daniel. III. Title.
NK2051. A1S54 1988
728'.09495   88-4067
ISBN 0-517-56874-8
10 9 8 7 6 5 4 3 2 1
First Edition

ACKNOWLEDGMENTS

We are particularly grateful to Yorgos Zaphiriou, an enthusiastic, efficient, warm, and welcoming guide and friend, as well as to Manolis Pantelidakis and Malin Alberg; Yannis Averof; Marcienne Beloeuvre; Marie-Claude Berard; Pierre Bodin; Olga and Stefanos Bulgaris; Andy Bylo; Catherine, Martin, and Simon de Chabaneix; Beatrice and Simeon Colin; Bacha and Maris Embiricos; Yannis Frangakis; Takis Frangoulis; Constantin Frontzos; Nicholas Gage; Yannis Galatis; Dolly Goulandris; Myriam and Pascal Herold; Danae Karacosta; Marilyn Karp; Katy and Pavlo Kremezis; Madeleine de Lamotte; Maro and Yannis Layia-Zeppos; Mercedes and Nick Malliotis; Yves Marbrier; Françoise and Jean-Marie Merillon; Eva Metzell; Clotilde Millies; Jean Moreau; Paola Navone; Andrew Pettit; Michel and Melpo Photiadis; Yo Remy Jensen; Lazare Rozensztroch; Catherine, Marcel, and Muriel Sabaton; Jonathan Scott; Marietta Sgourdaiou; François and Josette Sommaripas; Manos Sommaripas; Michael Steinberg; Vassilis Tseghis; Doda and Felix Voridis; Michael Ward; Maurice White; Catherine Willis; Françoise Winter; Dyllia Zannettos; and Damianos Zarifis.

We would also like to thank Harry Mark Petrakis, Panos Foscolos, and Laura Tagliavini; the Laboratoire Dupon; Ian Hammond; and Liz Gibbons. We are also grateful to our agent, Lucy Kroll and her associate, Barbara Hogenson; and Nancy Novogrod and Lauren Shakely, our editors at Clarkson N. Potter. Also we are thankful for the continued support of Alan Mirken and Bruce Harris of Crown Publishers; Carol Southern, publisher of Clarkson N. Potter; as well as Jonathan Fox; Maria Bottino; and Teresa Nicholas.

Suzanne Slesin, New York;
Stafford Cliff, London;
Daniel Rozensztroch, Paris;
Gilles de Chabaneix, Paris.
February 1988.

CONTENTS

FOREWORD

More than twenty years ago, Daniel Rozensztroch fell in love with Greece, and his affection for the land and the people helped inspire this book. Although less familiar with Greece we have nonetheless attempted to convey his enthusiasm and passion.

A third-class boat ticket, Marseilles to Piraeus, gift of a generous older brother as a reward for final exams (just barely) passed. Not yet the epoch of jet charters, the trip lasts three days, a stopover in Naples and a visit to Pompeii included as a bonus. Then the canal of Corinth, a narrow tunnel of rock opening into the Aegean Sea. Debarkation in Athens's lively port, already made famous by the film Never on Sunday. *From there, knapsack on my back, myths and mythologies on my mind, archaeological sites on my itinerary: of course, the Acropolis, Delphi, Mycenae, and Epidaurus. The classic route for students of Greek antiquity. But almost immediately, distractions—the indescribable light, the serenity of certain locations, the conviviality of the inhabitants. The discovery of a people—a joy, a birth of love, and a desire to become acquainted. Old women dressed in black, brawling children, men incessantly fingering worry beads, young people singing* rembetika. *First glimpse of the islands, glaringly white, well-balanced villages, the simplicity of the houses. What a lesson in architecture.*

A room in a local house, the sea lapping against thick walls in the shadows of windmills. Winding journeys through side streets and along donkey tracks, my indiscreet eye a voyeur of interiors. A blue door, slightly ajar. Whitewashed walls, a floor of slate flagstones, a colorful kourelou *thrown over a stone bench, an enormous jar.*

That day, although I didn't realize it then, must have been decisive in my life. Years later, when I became an interior designer, my tastes always ran more toward simplicity and authenticity than toward luxury and ostentation. This remains true today. I have returned to Greece nearly every year for the past twenty years. I have discovered the Dodecanese islands, those of the Ionian Sea, as well as the north of Greece, wooded and mountainous. Great friendships have been born; to love a country is to love its people.

I have often thought of the little house on Mykonos, encountered with such enthusiasm during my adolescence, when my tastes were still forming. As an adult I sought out my own little white house, which I found on another of the Cycladic islands. Whitewashed with lime in the local fashion, *koureloudes* scattered on the slate floor. I ensconced myself in an intimate and secluded spot, a faraway and solitary refuge, but also a shared vacation home. The amenities scarce and life archaic. Furniture dragged out of Athenian flea markets, shipped with great difficulty to the island, and hauled by mule up steep hills to the house. Friends contributing culinary talents to make the best use of the meager produce offered by the village grocers. The water supply precarious, the town washhouse replacing the private bath during the dry season. Yet harmony supersedes needs, and the value of time replaces frenzy. What a surprise to the blasé city dweller to see the baker wall up his oven with clay for each

day's baking. Others prefer places more civilized and accessible, the assistance of a fashionable decorator in the arrangement of the home. Yet what magic to realize that beauty and proportion are not measured against learning, except perhaps the ancestral and intuitive knowledge of a local mason whose initiative can grant new life to a house that has almost decayed into an old pile of stones.

The houses that move me the most are always marked by time, memory, use, and the events of life; old family houses run down for lack of means; modest, simple, common people's homes, sometimes transformed for another style of living. For me, it is humility and modesty that produce true richness and sometimes true sophistication.

To love a country is to love a people, but also its habits, customs, and houses. This book is not a historical summary, nor a traditional architectural thesis. It is simply the preferred route of travelers in love with Greece, with frequent stops to explore interiors that convey culture and identity – these houses, witnesses to Greek life.

Daniel Rozensztroch

ABOVE AND RIGHT: Behind the walls of the castle, the acropolis, one of the most dramatically sited in Greece, towers above the village, as dusk falls on Líndos.

INTRODUCTION

The lovely, haunting Greek word *nostalgia,* its meaning more poignant than the word conveys in English, was an emotion pervading my childhood. I was born in America, the fifth of six children, while my father, mother, and four older brothers and sisters were born on the island of Crete. As the songs, poems, and memories of their island passed from my parents to me, I felt myself an exile from that land where tall cypresses cast long shadows across the graves of my ancestors.

I was forty years old when I traveled to Greece for the first time, fearful that the firmament I had fashioned about the land I had never seen might be diminished by the reality. But the trip affirmed everything I had believed. In each of seven trips I have made to Greece since then, those first impressions have been strengthened. The regenerative quality of Greece, I understand now, isn't limited to those of Greek descent. Even strangers who visit Greece leave finding themselves in love with a vision that embraces past and present, a sense of place not clearly defined.

In the beginning there is the light of the sun reflected from mountains and sea with such incandescence that it may surpass light anywhere else in the world. Under that blazing sun, days are replete with stunning sights. The magic and force of that sun carries into the flower-laden and sea-scented fragrance of the night when one feels the myths and history seething and alive.

Olive groves and vineyards; on the tossing waves of the sea, the red hulls of boats. Etched in the faces of people the marks of struggle, sorrow, endurance. Rituals of planting and harvest, songs and dances, changeless in their essence from the time of Homer. The

LEFT: The facade of the Taxiarchos chapel within the walled monastery on Sériphos is of chiseled marble.

plaintive strains of a reed flute plays the music Odysseus might have heard while fishermen, casting their nets on a beach at twilight, could be descendants of his companions.

Wherever one travels across Greece, the past is a living presence. One feels it at Mycenae on an overcast day such as the somber one that awaited Agamemnon when he returned from Troy to be murdered by his wife, Clytemnestra. One hears it at dusk in Delphi with the voices of old oracles rising in the wind from the hidden gorges. (What are the voices saying? The Greeks believed each man and woman is destined to hear from the oracles what he or she wishes or fears

Entering a mountain village on the day of a wedding, the people in their finery, sharing whatever they have no matter how meager. In Greek the root word of hospitality, *filoxenia,* and friend, *filo,* is the same. After the ceremony in the small whitewashed church, the wedding celebration: the bride — lovely as Helen of Troy might have been — leading a line of girls in a dance, her black eyes flashing, her frock whipping about her slim ankles.

Hours later, the celebrants dispersed, the bride and groom cloistered away, I was awakened by the rumble of thunder, an ominous reverberation that rolled on and on like the cannonade of some epic battle. Standing at the window, I saw in the moonlight a grove of olive trees resembling gnarled old crones like the women in black who had been at the wedding. Silent and unsmiling they were a reminder that youth, love, and beauty fade and end in the embrace of death.

One of the joys of journeying in Greece is to climb a mountain path and from each plateau to look down, more and more of the landscape and seascape visible, until on peaks like Santorini and Monemvasia, one feels a spectator to a view of all the earth.

Resting for a while beside a mountain spring, the sounds of water teasing one's thirst. Then to cup one's palms, feel the cool water, and drink as men once drank before they fashioned tools, the water soothing tongue and throat and splashing eyes, cheeks, and chin.

To sleep in the utter stillness of night in a sheltered hamlet, stars hidden by crags and peaks so one feels the "fabulous, formless darkness" of Yeats. The first stirrings of the day, creeping stealthily upon its adversary, night, the darkness unwilling to relinquish its power as the light seeks dominance. Against the mystical unfoldments of Greece, one divines here the terror and beauty within the word we call *dawn*.

In the ancient ampitheater at Epidaurus, the plays of Aeschylus, Sophocles, and Euripides can still be watched in the glow of torches, a scene unchanged in its essence for centuries. At Thermopylae, the site of the pass where Leonidas and his three hundred Spartans fought to the death against the hordes of Persia, flowers bloom among the stones. As witness to the Greek penchant for spareness and beauty in their language as well as in the way they built their temples, on the site of that valiant battle, the austere lines, "Stranger, go and tell the Lacedaemonians that we lie here in obedience to their laws."

The mountains dividing Greece from the north have slowed but never stopped the endless invasions.

The land has been wracked by wars from the time of Homer. Alexander the Great, the legions of Rome, Franks, Venetians, Turks, Fascists, and Nazis, all sustained their tyranny for a while but, in the end, retreated. The people return to their labor from dawn to dusk, through all seasons, struggling for a minimal existence from the inhospitable earth.

The longest anguish and despair in the history of Greece were the four hundred years of slavery they endured under the Ottoman Turks, from the fall of Byzantium in 1453 until they won their freedom in 1830 after ten years of savage war. Those centuries of slavery have left a strain of sorrow in the Greek spirit. To understand modern Greece, one must understand the meaning of those centuries of slavery. Babies born, growing through childhood to adulthood, sometimes surviving to become old men and old women, living all their lives as slaves. Generation after generation of slavery for a people to whom the word *freedom* is as holy as the word *bread*.

If Greece has flowered in its art, philosophy, and drama, and if it has suffered through invasions, famines, and civil wars, it is the poets of Greece who explore and define its glory and its tribulation. They write of the sun, of the burden and challenge of the past, of restlessness and pilgrimages, of meditations, deaths, and resurrections. While loving their land as much as poets of other

ABOVE LEFT AND ABOVE: In the spring, the hills of Sériphos are covered in flowering thyme and lavender; the beaches are deserted.

countries love their own, a perception of vision allows the Greek poets to look beyond their own mountains, measuring their responsibilities to all mankind. At the end of the nineteenth century, the poet Kostas Palamas could write:

The Greek poet who has before him the example of his immortal ancestors, must be first of all a human being and must understand that true national poetry is poetry without a country and poetry in its highest intensity.

Palamas was a forebear of the Greek Nobel poet George Seferis who writes:

The free man, the just man, the man who is the "measure of life," if there is one basic idea in Hellenism, it is this one.

In his novel *Zorba the Greek*, Nikos Kazantzakis, the greatest of the modern Greek poets, shows us that even as Zorba relishes life, singing, dancing, drinking, and loving, he sees the stark specter of the skull beneath the face and recognizes the frailty and mortality of all men and women. Once a hater of Turks, Zorba comes to recognize there are good and evil Turks as there are good and evil Greeks. Finally, he acquires a wisdom that divines good and evil as human postulations. To be human, Zorba and the Greeks comprehended, is to encompass in every man and woman, good and evil, weakness and strength, sorrow and joy, life and death.

Against this mythic, cultural, and historical fecundity, we view the houses and gardens of Greece. Stone habitations warmed by the proliferation of bright flowers and colorful fabrics, winding over balconies and across trellises, adorning the starkness of stone and the stony earth. Decorations fuse the influences of Frankish, Venetian, and Turkish occupations. Each shuttered window conceals a mystery.

Each piece of furniture has a story. All stories bound irrevocably to the past, to the necromantic centuries. A continuity of time that extends even to the bed in which one is born and in which one dies, a bed for birth and a bed for death.

Before death, there is life. The poet celebrates that wonder and joy, as well. Odysseus Elytis, the second Nobel laureate of Greece, evokes a clear and simple testament:

Ah, life
Of a child who becomes a man
Always near the sea where the sun
Teaches him to breathe toward the place where
The shadow of a seagull vanishes.

Harry Mark Petrakis,
author of *A Dream of Kings* and *Collected Stories*

GREECE THE COUNTRY

The sun and the sea are Greece's principal resources and have been so

To arrive by boat in any port is dazzling and unforgettable. Piraeus, the port of Athens, was the most important harbor in the ancient world, and is now the most active in the Mediterranean. Today, such picturesque Greek pleasure harbors as Mykonos, Líndos, and Hydra reveal no perceptible distance from the country's seafaring past.

The islands of the Cyclades, with their whitewashed villages tumbling into the

since antiquity. In Greece, a country of fishing boats and freighters,

Aegean, and the Ionian Islands, trimmed with cypress and olive trees, present different aspects of a country of vividly contrasting views.

The lushness of green valleys vies with the austerity of parched lands, but the land and water provide a common thread. Even the *meltémi,* the summer wind that blows from the north, is perceived in varying ways. Considered the scourge of sailors, it is also the one element that brings a refresh-

ferries and yachts, one is never more than 90 kilometers from the sea.

ing coolness to the sunbaked villages of the islands.

OPPOSITE AND THIS PAGE: Boats – from simple fishing craft to modern cruise ships – are an intrinsic part of Greek life.

5

LEFT AND RIGHT: The Mediterranean to the south, the Ionian Sea to the west, and the Aegean Sea to the east offer more than 9,000 miles of coastline and 1,400 islands.

LEFT: The diverse landscapes of the Greek islands range from the wildflower-covered hills of Sériphos in the early spring, **FAR LEFT,** *to the austere cliffs of Santoríni in summer,* **BOTTOM LEFT.** *Thyme, oregano, rosemary, and wild lavender are some of the herbs that grow wild on the arid Cycladic islands,* **BELOW LEFT, BELOW FAR LEFT, AND BOTTOM FAR LEFT.** *Olive trees dot the mountains on Páros,* **LEFT.**

RIGHT: As the sun sets on Mykonos, balconies cantilevered over the water are silhouetted against the sky.

LEFT: In Greece, three colors predominate. White – the symbol of purity and cleanliness – is seen in the whitewashed facades that are repainted every year and the sidewalks that village women repaint every day. Blue – the color of the water, where all blues, turquoise to navy, are revealed – is repeated on windows and doors. Ocher – the color of earth, terra-cotta, and stone is the ever-present background. While popular houses tend to be starkly monochromatic, the more middle-class homes blend all the rich colors of the Orient.

LEFT: In the northern region of Epiros, a river flows through a lush valley of pine, poplar, and chestnut trees.

LEFT AND RIGHT: The light in Greece is legendary, luminous, dazzling, tangible, and infinite, revealing landscapes that are different – and somehow more extraordinary – each dawn or dusk. A shadow cast on a white mountaintop village and mountains nearly lost in an early-morning haze are varnished and perfected by the brilliant qualities of light.

LIVING IN GREECE

Men sitting at tables drinking tiny cups of dark coffee served with the

Today, the *kafeneion* and the *taverna*, public meeting places that replace the ancient *agora,* are still central to daily life in Greece, a country where strong traditions endure in spite of the push of modern times – and where women, seemingly eternally dressed in black, rule the home.

The calendar year is organized around the Greek Orthodox feasts and celebrations; religious customs are perpetuated by

traditional glass of water, playing cards or backgammon, or fingering

family traditions and sometimes imbued with a certain note of superstition. But the Greeks have not lost their sense of enjoyment. Music and dance remain an important way of expressing joy and pain.

OPPOSITE: The neoclassically decorated Café Neon on Athens's Omónia Square opened in 1924. It is one of the last political cafés of the city. Patrons sit facing the entrance to see the new arrivals.

komboloí and talking, talking, talking – mostly about politics and money.

THIS PAGE: Tavernas and kafeneions are at the center of social life throughout Greece.

LEFT AND RIGHT: *The Greeks, often blond and blue-eyed in the mountains, darker-skinned in the regions of strong oriental influence, all seem to exhibit the same pride and enthusiasm, serenity and joy.*

LEFT: The bustling activity of the Athenian fish market, set between majestic neoclassical colonnades, **LEFT,** contrasts with the sedateness of the fluorescent-lit interior of an old-fashioned notions emporium that dates from the 1930s, **BELOW LEFT.**

RIGHT: A hardware shop stocked with traditional Greek utensils, **RIGHT,** a family grocery, **BELOW RIGHT,** a store that specializes in ouzo, **BOTTOM RIGHT,** and one that offers only eggs, **TOP FAR RIGHT,** or olive oil and all kinds of olives, **CENTER FAR RIGHT,** and a fifties-style grocery filled with sweets, **BOTTOM FAR RIGHT,** are some of the small businesses that still flourish today.

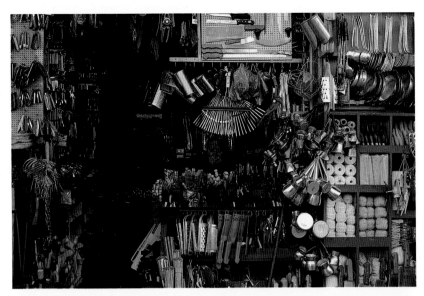

LEFT AND RIGHT: *Doors open onto gardens, lead into court-yards, or mark the entrance to the house. They are closed during the day to keep the interior cool. Usually made of wood and crowned with decorative flowers, brightly painted, or topped with a carved stone lintel, doors are symbols of Greek hospitality.*

The fear that the house will be touched by bad luck has resulted in a series of superstitions. Nailing a wooden cross blackened by candle smoke to the lintel, or placing, in May, a crown of flowers above the door is intended to protect the house from harm. The small over-the-door windows, in triangular or six-pointed star shapes, not only allow daylight to enter but are also meant to guard the house against the evil eye.

LEFT AND RIGHT: *Among the most striking examples of Greek neoclassicism are the many buildings in Athens, Nauplion, and Aegina that combine facades in the classical Hellenic style – decorated with columns, pilasters, and pediments – with pale ocher-hued colors that recall the palette of the Italian Renaissance. Athens, once a small village at the base of the Acropolis, was rebuilt in the early 19th century when the recently appointed ruler King Otho of Bavaria arrived with a number of architects. Ernst Ziller, who became one of the most important, came in the mid-1850s. The new city built in the neoclassical style became the capital of Greece in 1834.*

HOUSE STYLES

In Greece, people live in a great variety of buildings, from the naive

Whether they have walls whitewashed or covered in pastel-colored plaster, Greek houses are witnesses to a variety of rich cultural influences.

The stable family home with its strong heritage of generations of collecting is an interesting contrast to the centuries-old structures that are now being restored as summer houses. The contemporary point of view is uniting the avant-garde with the ancient. Folk-art traditions in which color

to the sophisticated, from the tiny cube-shaped island house to the grand

and pattern are used to enliven the plainest interior are inspiring a new generation of modernists.

Many Greeks who have traveled the world have returned home bringing with them an international life-style and a taste for modern luxury. Others tend to a more austere, meditative approach. Often choosing popular, even primitive houses, or remote islands, they adapt the rudimentary abodes into artistic

Italianate mansion situated on a vast estate or along an elegant avenue.

environments that are original expressions of personal taste.

OPPOSITE: A tin ex-voto representing a house is one of a series of symbolic images that wives of sailors brought to church for prayers of good fortune.

THIS PAGE: Houses, some with roofs of clay, some with flat roofs, are examples of the variety of architectural styles.

ARISTOCRATIC HERITAGE

Corfu, a lush and verdant island in the Ionian Sea, has over the past six centuries been under the influence of a number of rulers. The Venetians, French, English, and more recently the Italians have all left their mark on the island's houses. The eclectically sophisticated homes built by Corfu's successful merchants and landowners have remained in the same families for generations.

Stefanos and Olga Bulgaris are part of one of the oldest and most aristocratic families of the island. In the last few years, the couple has taken a new interest in their island's heritage.

ABOVE: The Italian-style house with its tile roof and stone steps is half hidden in a garden.

LEFT: Classic Italianate steps are at the entrance to the property.

ABOVE: *The alignment of the doors allows for an uninterrupted view through the main reception room of the house.*

ABOVE LEFT: *Vines climb up the trunk of a huge palm tree, which was planted long ago in the front garden.*

LEFT: *The plant-filled back garden is cool and shady.*

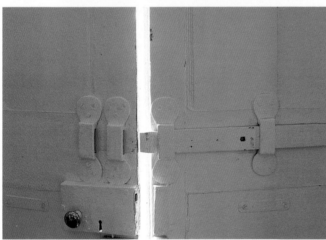

ABOVE AND RIGHT: The main reception room is furnished with a mix of English antiques, a grand piano, and a large Japanese watercolor.

LEFT: A huge bolt closes the front door.

FAR LEFT: *A collection of chiseled silver buckles and belts from northern Greece is displayed in a mother-of-pearl-encrusted vitrine.*

LEFT AND BELOW FAR LEFT: *The antique chess tables are signs of a foreign cultural heritage.*

BELOW LEFT: *Brought back to Corfu from Austria, the bent-wood rocker is the kind that was popular in Greece at the turn of the century.*

LEFT: *English and Italian antique dishes have been assembled in the dining room.*

RIGHT: *The antique carpet in the dining room is from the north of Greece. A screen hides the door to the kitchen.*

FAR LEFT: *The family's leather-bound books are stored in an antique Italian cupboard.*

LEFT: *A view of cypress trees can be glimpsed from the window.*

ABOVE: In the adjoining bedrooms, the wide-plank floor is highly waxed.

LEFT: The original elements of the huge kitchen have been retained by choice, with no attempt at modernization.

ABOVE: The iron and brass beds are reflected in the mirror of an old-fashioned English mahogany dressing table.

ART GALLERY
White marble and sculpted gold set the tone of the glittery gallery-like home that was the Athenian residence of Alexander Iolas, the internationally known art dealer who died last year. The Greek architect Dimitri Pikionis designed the monumental house with its palace-sized rooms for Iolas's collections of antique statuary and modern art.

ABOVE: *The low, contemporary house is set in a garden at the end of a marble walk.*

LEFT: *The fragment of a 12th-century Romanesque stone pillar on the porch is from Italy.*

LEFT: A collection of marble sculptures, including a Roman torso, has been assembled on the marble-paved terrace.

LEFT: Shutters are closed to protect the paintings within from the strong natural light.

ABOVE: A draped headless Roman figure, dating from the first or second century A.D., stands between two Roman columns. The marble window frame is modern.

TOP RIGHT: The wide stairway, with its marble balustrade inspired by antiquity, connects the garden to the second floor.

ABOVE RIGHT AND RIGHT: In the garden, Roman torsos have been placed in a colonnade of ancient stone fragments.

LEFT: *The two large contemporary bronze discs create a dramatic contrast with the paleness of the house.*

ABOVE: *Marble-walled rooms open onto one another on the ground floor.*

RIGHT: *Entwined leaves and flowers climb up the wrought-iron balustrade that was created by Claude Lalanne, a contemporary French sculptor.*

ABOVE: *The books in the marble-walled library have been covered in white paper.*

ABOVE LEFT: *The hammered-gold door is by Wolfgang Cardamatis, a Greek artist.*

LEFT: *Large paintings by the late American pop artist Andy Warhol, including a portrait of Alexander Iolas, dominate one of the gallery-like rooms. The seating elements are part of a 1969 furniture puzzle created by Sebastian Matta, a Chilean designer.*

ABOVE: The beds in the master bedroom have been placed one behind the other.

PAINTED HOUSE

Like many buildings in the mountainous northern region of Greece near the Albanian border, the house has had a turbulent history. Originally inhabited by a middle-class family, it was decorated in a neoclassical style fashionable at the beginning of the century. But the interior was completely destroyed in the early 20th century during the last months of the Turkish occupation.

The house's present owner has spent the last 20 years putting his personal touch on the decor. The result is a lively example of folk art.

ABOVE: The enthusiastic addition of color to the stone house contrasts with the somberness of the landscape.

LEFT: The current owner stands on the landing wearing a paint-stained shirt. On the wall is one of the paintings he created especially for the interior.

ABOVE: *The ornate balcony recalls the house's past.*

LEFT: *The neoclassical front door has been repainted in a naive trompe l'oeil wood pattern.*

LEFT: Every interior surface, from the ceiling moldings to the walls and doors, has been painted in strident color.

RIGHT: *Bright paint, trompe l'oeil textures, and decorative stencils are used to convey a folk-art interpretation of neo-classical detailing. Plastic flowers, vinyl flooring, gold-framed engravings, and a fifties hanging lamp are newly added details in the popular taste.*

ABOVE: *In a bedroom, the two wide mattresses are placed on either side of the stove in the oriental manner.*

LEFT: *The cupboard inset in the wall is typical of houses in the north of Greece.*

RIGHT: *Grapes are laid out on a cloth to dry on one of the beds in the spacious bedroom. A fireplace and a wood-burning stove are used to heat the room. A piece of fabric covers the fireplace opening during the warmer months.*

ISLAND RETREAT

In ancient times, Líndos, on Rhodes, in the Dodecanese islands, was one of the most important ports on the Aegean. The village also flourished during the Byzantine and medieval periods. An impressive 15th-century fortress built by the Knights of Saint John on the foundations of an ancient acropolis looms above the buildings of Líndos, which all exhibit strong medieval and Turkish architectural influences.

A few 17th-century houses that used to belong to ship captains remain. David Gilmour, the popular English rock musician, and his wife, Ginger, have renovated one of them as a summer home for their family.

ABOVE: *The Gilmour house in Líndos is at the foot of the fortress on Rhodes.*

LEFT: *A carved sandstone arch leads from the street to the private courtyard.*

ABOVE AND LEFT: Krokalia – *the black and white pebbles that are used in patterns both inside and outside the house – are traditional on Rhodes.*

LEFT: *Oleander, cactus, geranium, and banana plants grow in a variety of oversize terra-cotta pots in the courtyard and on the terraces of the house.*

RIGHT: *A Greek cotton tablecloth serves as a canopy to shade the long table, which is used for alfresco family meals.*

ABOVE: Wide steps encircle the entrance to the kitchen.

ABOVE: At the end of the sala, or main living room, a raised platform with mattresses functions as a summer bedroom.

RIGHT: In the evening, the pebble floor is covered with a rug, and cushions line the storage chests to provide comfortable seating for guests.

56

ABOVE: *Carved wood shutters frame a window that looks into the courtyard. The plaster motifs are oriental.*

RIGHT: *The chest, steps, banister, and platform of natural wood are traditional elements of Dodecanese interiors.*

ABOVE: *The master bedroom is at the top of the house. Indian pelmets hang on the windows, and a mosquito net from Ceylon is knotted over the bed.*

FAR LEFT: *Pink carnations are placed in a pottery pitcher from the island of Sámos.*

LEFT: *Israeli and local embroideries decorate the seating area in the main room. The low table, called a sofras, was originally used to serve Turkish coffee.*

POOLSIDE LUXURY

Pórto Ráfti, an ancient Mediterranean port, has become over the last 25 years a favorite residence for wealthy Athenians. Houses are situated on spectacular sites, with Olympic-size swimming pools, well-kept gardens, spacious outdoor terraces, and the staff to take care of it all.

Felix and Doda Voridis's contemporary stone house is a half-hour drive down the coast from Athens. A private chapel, beautiful garden, huge pool overlooking the Aegean, and open-air verandas, make this property the epitome of luxury.

ABOVE: *A private road sweeps through the property past the contemporary house.*

LEFT: *A large outdoor veranda extends the entertaining areas of the house.*

RIGHT: *The private chapel dedicated to Saint Paraskevi was built at the same time as the house. The frescoes are by Pavlos Samios.*

ABOVE: Near the pool, a table and chairs have been set up under bougainvillea.

RIGHT: The pool overlooks an awesome vista of the coastline.

CONCEPTUAL WORK

Although Manolis Pantelidakis's house on Sériphos in the Cycladic islands is the stage designer's summer home, it is also a conceptual work of art. Pantelidakis's approach is a response to the unique location of the whitewashed stone building, which is enveloped by a huge rock that is the base of a chapel.

Working as a sculptor, the artist has chiseled out the various living spaces, always preserving the powerful tactile quality of the natural rock. Nearly all the furnishings are the found objects that Pantelidakis has assembled more for their symbolic presence than for their function.

ABOVE: *An open courtyard that functions as a summer dining room is near the kitchen.*

LEFT: *A chapel sits on a rock above the house.*

RIGHT: *The interior courtyard, with its enormous arch of natural stone, is like a grotto.*

FAR LEFT: In a niche that was once a fireplace, a dressmaker's bust, found in Paris's Place des Vosges, is displayed as if in a lighted vitrine.

CENTER LEFT: A small studio area has been set up in front of a window on the ground floor.

LEFT: Reworking ship dioramas discovered in flea markets is a summer activity for the artist.

BELOW FAR LEFT: The three-part kitchen door allows for a play of light and shade.

BELOW CENTER LEFT: There is no glass in the windows of the tiny, minimally outfitted kitchen.

BELOW LEFT: The large round pebble placed on a piece of antique marble is a work of art by Manolis Pantelidakis. The handpainted glass advertising panels reflect an interest in found objects.

ABOVE RIGHT: Huge stones, driftwood, bits of wood paneling, and old pieces of luggage are the evocative furnishings of the ground-floor room.

RIGHT: The sleeping area of the ground-floor room is the only room in the house where natural rock is not visible. Instead, blocks of stone and marble have been integrated into the interior.

ABOVE: *On the upper floor, a window opens directly onto the rock wall.*

LEFT: *The staircase leading to a sleeping loft has been carved out of the rock and conceals a tiny bathroom. The old chair frame is like a sculpture.*

TOP RIGHT: *A black curtain theatrically controls the strong natural daylight in the bedroom. The bamboo, a traditional material for ceilings on Sériphos, is grown on the island.*

ABOVE RIGHT: *The bed platform has been positioned to provide views of the port, the sea, and the sky. A lantern from a Greek Orthodox church rests against the rock ledge.*

RIGHT: *An old wood door painted by Pantelidakis leans against one of the walls.*

THE FAMILY HOUSE

For many Greeks, there is nothing more important than the family.

When they do, they bring with them bounty and experiences from abroad. Establishing a stable base for future generations is primordial. In the 17th century, owing mostly to the flourishing trade with Venice, a new gentry emerged in Greece. Today, a few old families still possess the estates that their ancestors from that era willed to them. While some estates are in the process of disintegrating, slowly and graciously, others are energetically

Although they are by nature voyagers and adventurers, merchants,

being refurbished and kept alive.

English and Venetian furnishings, grand pianos, and libraries filled with leatherbound books are testimonies to the interests and culture of past generations, who had an open view of the world beyond and who always wanted to bring it all back home.

OPPOSITE: In a house in Ioanina, a town in Epiros in the north of Greece, a vintage

ships' captains, and pirates, they sooner or later will all return home.

photograph depicts three generations of an old and established family.

THIS PAGE: The grand houses of Greece reflect, in a range of styles, the enduring qualities of family life.

NOBLE RUIN

Originally from the north of Greece, the Kourkoumelli family moved to the island of Cephallonia to escape the Turkish invasion before establishing itself on Corfu. Their 400-year-old family house was built on the ruins of Corfu's 13th-century monastery at Afra. Set on a 2,000-acre estate, where olives were cultivated until the end of the 19th century, the building was constructed in four stages, the most recent of which is more than 200 years old.

English and Venetian furniture, heirloom silver, family portraits, and antique firearms recall a glorious history. The house has resisted the harsh climate, constant humidity, and time itself without losing its nobility and nostalgic charm.

ABOVE: *Majestic cypress trees dot the exuberant countryside on Corfu.*

LEFT: *A sculpted antique stone head sits on a wall on the Kourkoumelli estate.*

LEFT: *The valley stretches beyond the grounds of the family house.*

LEFT: *By the entrance to the property, metal troughs once held hay for the horses.*

73

RIGHT: On the rear facade of the house is a variety of shuttered windows.

BELOW RIGHT: The covered walkway leading to the house can be closed off with a wrought-iron gate.

BELOW FAR RIGHT: Peeling paint adds to the romantic appeal of the arched window.

OPPOSITE: The grand house, with its roof of Roman tiles and its walls of rough pink plaster, is in the classic Italianate style.

ABOVE: *A wide interior gallery opens onto the formal ground-floor rooms.*

LEFT: *The graceful arcade dates from the 13th century.*

ABOVE: *Colorful stained glass windows face the garden.*

RIGHT: *Originally part of the monastery, the stone arches were used for the foundations.*

ABOVE: *English and Chinese porcelain tea sets are stored in a glass-fronted mahogany cabinet that was imported from England in the 19th century.*

RIGHT: *The dining room is dominated by the 17th-century portrait of Matheos Rodostamo and portraits of two other Kourkoumelli ancestors. The bare, bleached wood floor contrasts with the elegance of the polished English furniture.*

RIGHT: Walking sticks and riding crops are kept on a rack in the gallery.

BELOW RIGHT: Old photographs and personal memorabilia that were collected by many generations of the Kourkoumelli family contribute to the masculine air of the study.

LEFT: The main sitting room takes up most of the ground floor. Leather-bound books in the glass-fronted bookcase and a majestic grand piano are evidence of the family's cultured way of life.

FAR LEFT: The huge portrait of Polimnias Scaramanga, a Kourkoumelli ancestor, was painted in Moscow at the beginning of the 19th century by the czar's personal portraitist.

LEFT: In the smaller, more intimate salon, lighting is provided by a Venetian-glass chandelier.

ABOVE: The anteroom outside the kitchen has a floor of paved stone. The old coffee mill and antique scale are still in use.

RIGHT: In the basement kitchen, the huge wood-burning hearth is made out of stone lined with ceramic tiles. A wooden plate-rack for drying dishes hangs above the stone sink. The centrally placed worktable has a thick stone top.

ON THE PORT

The small house that belongs to a fashion designer born on Mykonos is situated directly on the sea, within sight of Little Venice – an ancient fisherman's port where the buildings are raised on stilts.

With its whitewashed walls, painted ceilings and floors, and family heirlooms the house has been restored to recall the simple beauty of the past.

ABOVE: An exterior staircase with well-worn stone steps connects the different floors of the house. Geraniums grow in olive-oil cans that have recently been painted white.

LEFT: The windows and balcony on the facade that faces the sea were restored.

LEFT: *A ferry making its way back to Piraeus, the port of Athens, can be seen from the second-floor anteroom.*

ABOVE: *Lace curtains diffuse the light that enters through the large windows overlooking the balcony.*

LEFT: *Dark wood panels have been inserted in the walls separating the hall from the living room.*

ABOVE: All the rooms open onto the large hall, where the beamed ceiling and wood floor are painted blue.

ABOVE RIGHT: The arch at the end of the windowless dining room has been mirrored to give the illusion of extra space.

RIGHT: In the kitchen, decorative objects are displayed on the old cooking hearth, which is no longer in use.

FAR RIGHT: A corner of the living room is furnished with a 19th-century sofa that is typical of the Cycladic islands. The cushions are covered in a traditional woven cotton. The rug was also made in the islands.

PROTECTED ENVIRONMENT

Although particularly large, the house in Métsovo is the kind of structure found in the mountainous and rugged region of Epiros in the north of Greece. Dating from the 18th century, the family house was meant to shelter its inhabitants from Turkish invasions.

A simple, unadorned facade, small windows, and rough stone walls contribute to the rather forbidding and austere exterior. By contrast, the interior, with its fireplace and wall-to-wall banquettes, is warm and inviting, reflecting the influence of the oriental style.

ABOVE: The house has a view of the main street of Métsovo.

LEFT: For security, tiny windows line the side of the stone house.

LEFT: Huge cabbages grow in the garden that provides year-round vegetables for the family.

LEFT: An oriental painting on tin, an old samovar, and a collection of swords are grouped in the second-floor dining room.

BELOW LEFT: A platform over the staircase doubles as a table. Pitchers and copper plates are displayed along the polished wood molding.

RIGHT: The dining room is on the second-floor landing. Chairs dating from the 1920s have been upholstered with locally made wool fabric. A ladder is used to reach the attic.

LEFT: The living room has been furnished in a manner typical of the north of Greece. The ceiling is of carved wood; the fireplace, banquettes, carpet, and monumental copper brazier are Turkish in influence. Double windows provide insulation – a necessity in the cold and often snowy region.

RIGHT: A bleached wide-plank wood floor lines the second-floor bedroom hallway.

CENTER RIGHT: Local shepherds crafted the walking sticks.

FAR RIGHT: The ornate chair is a Greek interpretation of a turn-of-the-century English design. The motifs in the rug are characteristic of Epiros. On the inlaid wood desk is a series of inkwells that were used by itinerant scribes during the Turkish occupation.

BELOW RIGHT, CENTER RIGHT, AND FAR RIGHT: Weavings cover the pillows on the banquettes. Important family members are remembered in large formal paintings as well as in small, intimate photographs.

OLD-WORLD CHARM

Built directly on a massive rock, the Manessi house is isolated on a lush, hilly site overlooking the sea. It was once the center of a huge agricultural estate and is still inhabited by the descendants of an old Corfu family.

Venetian in influence, the house retains an atmosphere of old-world charm. Parts of the building were added on at different times and are connected by stairs, catwalks, and verandas. The private chapel, dedicated to the family's personal saint, is a sign of nobility.

ABOVE: The house seems to rise out of the verdant landscape of the island of Corfu.

LEFT: An English cast-iron chair stands on the veranda.

LEFT: Steep steps lead up to the main house, which was built to conform to the rocky site.

LEFT: The age of the house is reflected in the peeling layers of plaster and paint of the exterior.

ABOVE: *The veranda takes advantage of the breeze and the panoramic view.*

LEFT: *Terra-cotta pots are assembled on a wall in the garden.*

96

ABOVE: *The private chapel is just below the main house.*

LEFT: *In one of the estate's outbuildings, there is a room with beekeeping equipment.*

LEFT: The Greek Orthodox chapel is still used for private family ceremonies.

RIGHT: A wreath of flowers, symbolizing Mother Earth, is traditionally hung over the front door on the first of May.

FAR RIGHT: Garden hoses are attached to spigots on the neo-classical fountain.

BELOW RIGHT: A catwalk links the main house to one of the outbuildings.

BELOW FAR RIGHT: An arched stone doorway leads to the ancient olive grove.

BOTTOM RIGHT: The heavy front doors of the chapel are ornamented with iron crosses.

BOTTOM FAR RIGHT: Double sets of doors, one of solid wood, the other inlaid with colorful stained glass, are at the entrance to the main house.

LEFT: Family portraits hang near the fireplace in the living room.

BELOW LEFT: The piano in one of the small sitting rooms is a reminder of the strong musical traditions of the Ionian Islands.

RIGHT: The large desk is reserved for the head of the house.

CENTER RIGHT: To conserve heat, the staircase leading to the bedroom floor can be closed off with a wooden lid.

FAR RIGHT: In the kitchen, terracotta tiles top the old-fashioned wood- or coal-burning stove.

BELOW RIGHT: A beautifully time-worn mirror reflects an incense burner from a church.

BELOW CENTER RIGHT: From the living room, doors open directly onto the enclosed stairway of painted wood.

BELOW FAR RIGHT: On the kitchen table is a recent delivery of eggs fresh from the farm.

OFFICIAL RESIDENCE

Once the mayor of Ioánina, the capital of Epiros, Constantin Frontzos is considered a leading citizen of the northern city. Frontzos still lives in his parents' house, which is situated in the center of town. The sculpted ceilings, bright colors, and numerous decorative details – all Turkish in feeling – have been gracefully preserved.

ABOVE: Small stores and workshops in the tradition of the oriental bazaar can be found in the center of Ioánina.

LEFT: The townhouse is entered through a covered gallery.

LEFT: Constantin Frontzos poses in the office of his home. The two telephones are a sign of the ex-mayor's active life.

TOP: The brightly painted, carved wood cupboard has been highlighted in gold.

ABOVE: Once filled with coal, the mangali, a copper brazier, was used to heat the room.

TOP: A Venetian-glass chandelier hangs from the ceiling in one of the bedrooms.

ABOVE: In the dining room, the ceiling rosette is of boldly painted carved wood.

RIGHT: Multipatterned rugs cover the wide, low banquettes in the master bedroom. Used as either sofas or beds, the banquettes have been placed on either side of the carved stone fireplace. Pitchers are displayed in a series of niches that reflect their shape.

NEOCLASSICAL EXAMPLE

On Páros as on many other of the Cyclades sophisticated neoclassical residences built at the end of the last century stand with simple houses of fishermen and farmers.

The large residence in the main town, surrounded by a garden of lemon trees, is the island's most notable example of the refined neoclassical style. The generously proportioned rooms were furnished with pieces imported from the mainland, which were meant to reflect the urbane tastes of the late-19th-century bourgeoisie.

ABOVE: The strong colors of neoclassical houses create a contrast with the modest whitewashed houses.

LEFT: The neoclassical pediment of the house on Páros has been copied from an ancient temple.

LEFT: One of the hundreds of small chapels on the island has a dome that is tinted blue to symbolize the heavens. The trunks of the hibiscus trees have been whitewashed to protect them from insects.

107

ABOVE: *In the hall, straw hats hang on hooks on a trompe l'oeil painted stone wall.*

LEFT: *The doors at the entrance to the house are inset with colored glass panels.*

ABOVE RIGHT: *The hall floor is covered in a patterned ceramic tile.*

ABOVE CENTER RIGHT: *A graceful niche frames a bouquet of lilac.*

ABOVE FAR RIGHT: *The upstairs hall floor is of bleached wood.*

RIGHT: *Original bentwood chairs furnish the dining room.*

CENTER RIGHT: *The painted ceiling is in one of the reception rooms.*

FAR RIGHT: *Tall doors open into the pantry.*

 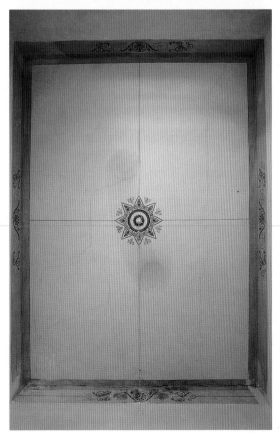 

ABOVE: In the main living room, velvet draperies are tied back with cotton cording.

FAR LEFT: An old-fashioned sofa and club chair sit directly on the terrazzo floor in the ground-floor waiting room.

LEFT: In a bedroom, the built-in closet with its large bottom drawer is typical of many Greek houses.

BELOW FAR LEFT: Upholstered furniture, heavy draperies, a large antique rug, and the ornately stenciled ceiling of the main living room are formal decorative elements that survive from the past.

LEFT: The Greek key motif is repeated in friezes that line the stenciled ceilings.

RIGHT: Interior shutters close off the tall windows in the main living room.

ABOVE: The white marble sink and drain board, the large hood over the cooking area, and the white ceramic tiles on the walls are details of an old-fashioned kitchen.

LEFT: Lemon trees grow in the back courtyard.

FAR LEFT: In the kitchen, a bowl of just-picked lemons has been set on the marble counter. Since antiquity, Páros has been known for its marble quarries.

113

RURAL TRADITION

Since its construction in 1617, the simple, rusticated house has been the home of the Lascaris family. It sits on a hill surrounded by olive groves, orange trees, and vineyards in San Marco, a tiny picturesque village of fishermen on Corfu.

The current occupants, members of the original family, used to live in Kérkira, the capital of the island, and visited the house only on weekends. Now retired, they have become permanent San Marco residents and are pursuing their passion for domestic and rural traditions.

ABOVE: *Access to the village house is through a heavy wood door set in a stone wall.*

LEFT: *The facade of the house, which overlooks the sea, is half hidden by luxuriant plantings. The arcade, high terrace, and terra-cotta tiled roof are of Venetian influence.*

LEFT: *The courtyard is paved with rough stones. A door leads to a cool storage room.*

LEFT: Century-old grapevines frame one of the doorways of the thick-walled house.

RIGHT: Lush tropical plants provide shade in the back garden.

CENTER RIGHT: The high-backed chairs on the terrace are made from recycled cast-iron stair railings.

FAR RIGHT: Grapevines add to the romantic feeling of the arcade.

BELOW RIGHT: A piece of local pottery stands on the veranda.

BELOW CENTER RIGHT: Once used for olive oil, the huge pottery jar is now a decorative element in the courtyard.

BELOW FAR RIGHT: A pillow in the shape of a bouquet of roses has been placed on a chair near pots of flowering geraniums.

LEFT: *In the summer, a simply crafted table and benches are used for dining on the veranda.*

LEFT: *A beamed wood ceiling and wide-plank floor dominate the comfortable living room.*

RIGHT: Bottles and casks of local wine, jars of olive oil, and fresh country hams are stored in the cool cellar.

RIGHT: A collection of old iron keys hangs above a stock of homemade jams and preserves.

FAMILY TIES

The Galatis family is one of the oldest and best-known on Mykonos. Many successive generations have lived in the lovely village house on the island. The present owner's enduring family ties are reflected in the marble fountain he had built to commemorate his mother.

Since her death, nothing has been changed in the house. The old-fashioned furnishings, antique lace, and numerous knick-knacks that fill the rooms also keep her memory alive.

ABOVE: *Grapevines grow on the terrace of the village house.*

LEFT: *The decorative fountain near the front door is dedicated to the family matriarch.*

LEFT: A second-floor bedroom opens directly onto the terrace.

ABOVE: *A dressing table stands in a corner, near a naively painted family portrait.*

LEFT: *The ornate marble corner fireplace has been whitewashed. Alternating panels of blue and white glass are inset into the balcony doors.*

ABOVE: *In the living room, an old-fashioned oil lamp is reflected in the antique mirror hung over a chest inlaid with mother-of-pearl.*

ABOVE RIGHT: *A porcelain bowl and pitcher that were once used for washing now stand decoratively on the grand piano.*

RIGHT: *Signs of prosperity, mirrors hang on every wall in the living room.*

ABOVE: *A collection of plates decorates the wall above the sink in the combination kitchen and dining room.*

RIGHT: *A pot for making coffee, an incense burner, and a cruet set are objects found in every traditional Greek home.*

TERRACED HOUSE

With its colorful history linked to the exploits of pirates, sailors, and shipowners, Hydra is a sophisticated island where many old families have strong roots. The austere whitewashed house that dominates the port from the heights of the island was once a ship captain's home.

Admirably sited on rocky terrain, the house has a multitude of small terraces that are accidents of the natural landscape. The interior is a mix of locally crafted pieces and stylish furnishings that were imported from abroad.

ABOVE: The captain's house has a wide view over the port of Hydra. The imposing houses close to the water were once pirate dwellings.

FAR LEFT AND LEFT: Set in thick stone walls, the windows have interior shutters.

ABOVE: *Apricots are laid out to dry in the sun on the steps built into the rocks.*

LEFT: *The front door opens onto a wide flagstone terrace with a panoramic view of the village and its tiled roofs.*

LEFT: Sunlight plays softly on a wicker chair.

RIGHT: Small windows punctuate the stark facade that faces the sea.

FAR RIGHT: Semicircular stone steps mark the entrance.

BELOW RIGHT: A terrace overlooks the mountain.

BELOW FAR RIGHT: Off a tiny path, a door opens onto the shaded patio.

BOTTOM RIGHT: The brilliant purple hue of the bougainvillea contrasts with the subtle tones of the dry and rocky terrain.

BOTTOM FAR RIGHT: The high-walled terrace, with its white-painted wrought-iron furniture, is a pleasant place to sleep under the stars.

FAR LEFT: *The smooth flagstone floor contributes to the coolness of the interior. The settee was made on the islands.*

LEFT: *A pillow placed on the floor allows the spectacular view from the front door to be appreciated, even when talking on the telephone.*

BELOW FAR LEFT: *The wall-hung dish rack is the focal point of the renovated kitchen.*

BELOW CENTER LEFT: *Narrow steep stairs lead to the large living room on the floor above.*

BELOW LEFT: *Once the attic of the house, the sparsely furnished living room has an exposed-wood ceiling.*

RIGHT: *The deep arched windows, dark wood floor, beamed ceiling, and unadorned white walls give the bedroom its monastic air. The bed is a superb example of Thonet bentwood from the turn of the century.*

REMINDER OF THE PAST

Nauplion, a town on the Peloponnesian coast, was the official capital of Greece from 1829 to 1834. The numerous 19th-century neoclassical buildings are reminders of the town's aristocratic roots.

Originally built for one of the town's most important families, the majestic three-story house faces the port from the main square. Little has changed in the house over the years, except for the poetic layering of objects and mementos from the family's past.

ABOVE: The neoclassical house stands on the main square of Nauplion. Exterior shutters shield the interior from the sun and heat of the day.

LEFT: The ground floor is made up of storerooms.

LEFT: A sweeping circular stair-case connects the two residential floors of the mansion.

ABOVE: *In the main reception room, each of the ceiling coffers has been painted in a different floral motif.*

LEFT: *A variety of styles and periods is reflected in the intriguingly eclectic furnishings of the living room.*

ABOVE RIGHT, ABOVE CENTER RIGHT, AND ABOVE FAR RIGHT: *Personal memorabilia, old master paintings, antique silver, and cut-glass decanters are arranged on the walls and shelves.*

RIGHT: *The upright piano was an essential part of the bourgeois interior.*

CENTER RIGHT: *A bare bulb hangs in the hall outside the living room. The wainscoting has been painted in trompe l'oeil marble.*

FAR RIGHT: *Everyday objects are assembled on a sideboard.*

134

RIGHT: In another bedroom, an antique samovar stands on a white ceramic stove. Although dilapidated, the room exudes a romantic atmosphere.

LEFT: *In the small room near the kitchen, freshly repainted cupboards store provisions.*

BELOW LEFT: *A plastic tub and an old colander are still in service in the kitchen.*

RIGHT: *The housekeeper reads the local paper sitting at the vinyl-covered table in the kitchen. Bottled gas has replaced wood or coal for the stove. Against the wall is a basic version of the traditional Greek dish rack.*

CRAFTED IN WOOD

The spacious residence in Mét-sovo that belongs to a collector of popular arts and crafts has been carefully restored according to the mountain village's architectural heritage. Because of the nearby forests, wood is an abundant and favored building material. The main reception rooms of the house have been expanded by the addition of an enclosed balcony, which is cantilevered over the street.

ABOVE: Nineteenth-century porcelain figurines represent the king and queen of Greece in national dress.

LEFT: Double cantilevered balconies with rows of windows extend the interior space.

RIGHT: In the oriental manner, rugs are hung on the wall, used to cover the banquettes, and made into pillows. The patterns and colors of the woven-wool rugs are typical of Epiros.

RIGHT: The coffered ceiling in the main room of the house has been left unpainted.

FAR RIGHT: A hammered copper tray on a base functions as a low table by the fireplace.

BELOW RIGHT: In the pantry, mountain herbs dry on simple pine shelves that hold examples of rustic antique pottery.

LEFT: A banquette stretches across the room under the un-usual double row of windows in the main reception space.

143

THE POPULAR HOUSE

The vernacular buildings that still exist in Greece, whether on the

The *hora,* or village, was made up of a group of buildings set at the top of the hill, often near a fortress that could shield the local people from foreign invaders.

On the islands, small chapels topped by round blue cupolas still add a touch of vibrant color to the all-white villages. Narrow donkey paths lined with pebbles or large whitewashed stones snake through the towns. Tiny houses with overhanging wood balconies and exterior

mainland or on the islands, were once inhabited by modest farmers

stone staircases are piled one atop the other in an intricate pattern.

On the mainland, in the north of Greece, the life of the family is centered around the fireplace, the only source of heat in the *sala,* the main living room that is also used for sleeping. Mattresses are traditionally placed on either side of the fireplace. On the islands, the bedroom is kept apart from the rest of the house. The bed is considered sacred and is proudly

or fishermen and still retain the simplicity and modesty of their origins.

decorated with the family's finest linens and embroideries.

OPPOSITE: Rustic folding chairs stand below a row of popular printed images.

THIS PAGE: Made of stone, wood, or plaster, the popular house in Greece has a simple, timeless charm.

RUGGED EXTERIOR

Near the border of Albania, in the north of Epiros, there are many small villages that date from the Turkish occupation. The houses, often hundreds of years old, were built solely as shelters. Everything is made of stone – from the village paths to the walls and roofs of the buildings, which were meant to blend in with the rugged monochromatic landscape.

Like other village houses, the large house in Monodéndri has interiors that reflect an elaborately decorative Turkish influence in its painted ceilings, colorful textiles, and the stucco fireplaces that were as necessary in the harsh mountain climate as they were ornamental.

ABOVE: Monodéndri is a mountain village north of the town of Ioánina in the Epiros region.

LEFT: The roof and walls of the large house are entirely made of local stone. Only the rooms on the second floor were lived in by the family. The ground floor was for storerooms and stables.

LEFT: *The eaves that support the roof of the house are carved of stone. No cement was used in the construction of the walls.*

LEFT: *The narrow track in the middle of the steep stone path matches the wheel span of the donkey-drawn carts that once made their way through the village. The wide stones by the doorways serve as benches.*

FAR LEFT: *Inside the front door, a staircase leads up to the family's living area. Wood partition walls divide the ground-floor stockrooms.*

LEFT: *The kitchen is suspended above the stairs.*

BELOW FAR LEFT: *Thick walls and small windows protected with iron bars are characteristic of the local houses.*

BELOW LEFT: *Wood shutters insulate the interior from the cold.*

LEFT: The panels covering the walls were once painted with decorative motifs. The current occupants have added a family photograph to the decor.

BELOW LEFT: The wood paneling in one of the second-floor bedrooms encloses a built-in cupboard, a shuttered window, and the door.

BOTTOM LEFT: A folk-art painted chest stands in the entrance hall, which is paved with thick irregular stones.

RIGHT: A bedroom furnished in the oriental manner is shared by many members of the family.

RIGHT: An extra bed has been added to one of the bedrooms. Pieces of fabric cover the fireplace during the months when it is not in use.

RIGHT: In the small kitchen, the bright red walls, yellow butane gas tank, turquoise-painted stone sink, and patterned vinyl tablecloth reflect a feeling of spontaneity and vitality.

HILLSIDE HAVEN

Francois and Josette Somma-ripas – he is a Greek journalist, she is a French weaver – moved to the Cycladic island of Sériphos 14 years ago. The couple lives in a popular village house set on a hill, which is exposed to the rugged north wind that blows during most of the year. Very few changes were made to the original structure, once the refuge of the famous Greek war-time aviator Nikos Primikyris.

ABOVE: A bird's-eye view of the house shows that it is organized around a courtyard and terrace.

LEFT: The exterior wall acts as a barrier to the wind and precipitous terrain. Inset windows take advantage of the view.

LEFT: *At the end of the house, adjacent to the terrace, stands an old pigeon house, a typical island structure.*

LEFT: *Built on rock, the house is entered through a narrow court-yard. Steps that are part of a public path lead to a study.*

ABOVE: *A door closes off the wood stove when it is not in use in the tiny kitchen.*

ABOVE LEFT: *Nineteenth-century antiques contrast with the rustic look of the bedroom's walls and floor.*

LEFT: *François Sommaripas uses one of the rooms as a writer's retreat.*

RIGHT: *An old-fashioned coffee grinder is attached to the rough marble top of the dining room table. The handcrafted café chairs are typically Greek.*

OLD COUNTRY

In the countryside outside the town of Rhodes, many villages still remain where elderly people live according to the customs of their ancestors.

In the village of Lahania, an old woman has proudly and carefully displayed all her precious possessions in the living room of her small house.

ABOVE: In her rose garden, the old woman in traditionally somber dress is a picture of serenity.

LEFT: An arched doorway opens onto the rose garden.

ABOVE: The bread oven is on the outside of the house.

ABOVE LEFT: Embroideries, laces, and religious images are meticulously arranged on the walls of the living room. The wide arch that divides the room is typical of Dodecanese houses.

LEFT: By comparison with the orderly living room, the family bedroom, with its rumpled bedclothes and haphazardly hung pictures, is in disarray.

TRADITIONAL FARMHOUSE

Perivola is the name of the house that was built on the island of Aegina in 1780 by Georges Bulgari, the governor of the neighboring island of Hydra. Constructed on an ancient archeological site, the farmhouse is part of a 100-acre pistachio plantation – the nuts are a crop for which Aegina is internationally renowned. One of the oldest houses on the island, the building has not changed since the 18th century.

ABOVE: *Both the arched door and window of the farmhouse kitchen have been painted red.*

LEFT: *A huge bougainvillea nearly covers the entire wall in the courtyard.*

RIGHT: *One of the entrance gates to the property is closed off with an enormous old bolt.*

TOP: *A wreath of dried flowers hangs over the front door as a symbol of good luck.*

ABOVE: *In the stone-paved entrance hall, a rustic staircase leads to the bedrooms.*

RIGHT: *An old master painting portraying an elderly Greek woman stands out against the whitewashed wall.*

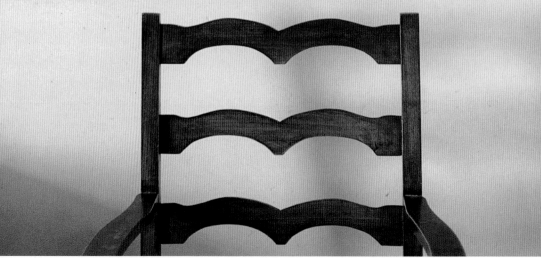

ABOVE: *Pillows covered in traditional weavings are piled on a settee crafted on the island.*

LEFT: *The living room of the rusticated farmhouse is simply but elegantly furnished.*

163

RIGHT: *The pink-tiled bathroom is a modern addition.*

FAR RIGHT: *In the bedroom, a box sits on a rug covering a storage chest that is decorated in an etched design.*

BELOW RIGHT: *As in many Greek houses, an oil lamp burns in front of an altar with icons.*

SOPHISTICATED STATEMENT

Originally the modest home of a sailor in the 19th century, the house on the island of Hydra has been renovated by a young restaurateur who lives there year-round.

Set on a hill overlooking the port, the building features a lovely interior courtyard and a spacious terrace. The thick whitewashed stone walls, wide-plank floors, and painted wood ceilings recall the house's traditional beginnings. But the tastefully chosen furnishings convey a sense of contemporary European refinement.

ABOVE: *Houses climb up the rocky hillside above Hydra.*

LEFT: *An old door-latch opens the front door of the house.*

LEFT: On the terrace, a white cotton hammock offers a spectacular view. The pot of fragrant basil is traditional.

LEFT: The well-planted courtyard contrasts with the island's arid and barren landscape.

ABOVE: *French doors open onto the kitchen.*

RIGHT: *The combination kitchen and dining room has a floor of painted concrete and a beamed wood ceiling. Water is stored in a stone cistern. An enameled ceramic stove heats the room.*

ABOVE: *A piece of antique, lace-trimmed white linen is used as a curtain on the door of a bedroom.*

RIGHT: *The bright blue shutters are closed during the day to help diffuse the light in the all-white bedroom.*

ABOVE: *On the second-floor landing, an old-fashioned lamp hangs from the painted wood ceiling.*

LEFT: *Mosquito netting is draped over the copper-frame bed in the sparsely furnished master bedroom.*

171

ORIENTAL INSPIRATION

The mosques and minarets in the old district of Ioánina in Epiros date from the time when the town was occupied by the Turks. Although years ago there were also many private houses inspired by oriental architecture, few remain today.

Ioánina was liberated from the Turks in 1913. The large house that still survives from the occupation once accommodated the owner's harem, but is now inhabited only by a watchman and his family.

ABOVE: *The house is one of the few remaining examples of Turkish-influenced architecture.*

LEFT: *The watchman contemplates a scale model, which he crafted himself, of the house.*

LEFT: In the center of Ioánina stands a mosque and minaret built when the town was under Moslem rule.

LEFT: The minaretlike bell tower of a church near Ioánina marks the importance of oriental architecture in the area.

ABOVE: A deep arch opens onto a ground-floor gallery. The table and chairs are set up for coffee.

RIGHT: On the second floor, a bird cage can be glimpsed through the decoratively shaped window.

ABOVE: *The heavy metal-studded door separates the house from the street. The plaque bears the owner's name.*

LEFT: *Graduated wide steps descend from the galley to the cellar. The terra-cotta jar is used to store olive oil.*

RIGHT: Laundry is hung out to dry in the cavernous ground-floor gallery.

176

ABOVE: The current life of the house is concentrated in one room where two worlds coexist. A modern gas heater has been placed in front of the Turkish fireplace. A new upholstered sofa is next to one of the oriental banquettes, and an electrical conduit runs along the wood-paneled ceiling.

WORLD'S END

South of the city of Salonika, in Macedonia, the stone house called *elia,* or olives, is situated at the end of the peninsula of Sithonía in the village of Nikiti. Set directly on the rocky shore, the house gives the impression of being located at the end of the world.

Maro Laya, a dealer in modern art, uses the former fisherman's dwelling as a primitive retreat from civilization. The interior is furnished with only a few basic elements for living – tables, chairs, and beds.

ABOVE: *A terrace faces the sea and rocky shore.*

LEFT: *Tiny windows, set into a fortresslike facade as protection against the elements, recall the building's past.*

RIGHT: *The house stands like a sentinel on the promontory.*

ABOVE: A mattress softens the roughness of the stone bench in front of the house.

RIGHT: Slitlike windows overlooking the sea are set into thick walls in the monastic bedroom.

BELOW RIGHT: The master bedroom has the luxury of a fireplace.

ABOVE: Pomegranates create a vibrant composition.

LEFT AND BELOW LEFT: A wooden hut near the main house serves as a summer bedroom.

ABOVE: *An old-fashioned oil lamp, now electrified, is a link between the past and present.*

LEFT: *The spacious ground floor of the house includes a living room and bedroom raised on a platform. White cotton curtains can be drawn for privacy.*

LEFT: *In the winter, only a primitive iron stove heats the ground floor.*

ABOVE AND RIGHT: The kitchen, with its slate counter and deep-set window, has no modern conveniences beyond bottled gas.

INGENUOUS APPEAL

The two-story cube-shaped structure on Mykonos is typical of many island village houses. Situated on a narrow street, the house looks much like its neighbors. The new concrete balcony that replaced the graceful old wooden one is an example of the rush to modernization.

Despite the wood-paneled ceiling, the elaborate moldings that give the interior a bourgeois tone, and the fanciful furnishings, the house has retained an ingenuous charm.

ABOVE: On Mykonos, the main village is unusually situated at the port. The island is famous for its windmills.

LEFT: The window frames, shutters, and front door of the village house have been painted gray, a traditional color on Mykonos.

LEFT: *The beamed wood-paneled ceiling includes a center rosette typical of northern Greece.*

BELOW FAR LEFT: *The tiny bedroom is furnished with a traditional antique copper bed.*

BELOW LEFT: *The dining and living rooms are adjacent. Lace cloths cover both tables.*

BOTTOM FAR LEFT: *A votive lamp hangs between the two antique gilded mirrors in the living room.*

BOTTOM LEFT: *Blue and white china is displayed in a painted folk-art cabinet.*

RIGHT: *The all-white pantry has a slate-tile floor. Dishes are kept in the wall cupboard; scalloped lace decorates the high shelf; and olive oil is stored in the huge pottery jars.*

ISLAND HIDEOUT

Originally, the modest Cycladic house on Sériphos was a hideout for pirates who stowed their booty under the wide-plank floors. Now, it is the home of Danae Karakosta, a painter who has decided not to change anything in the small house that would detract from its characteristic simplicity.

ABOVE: A rag rug covers part of the wide-plank floor in the main room of the house. Mattresses with natural-wool spreads woven on Mykonos are set on raised wood platforms and function as both sofas and beds.

LEFT: The house is made up of a series of cubic elements that overlap with their neighbors.

ABOVE: *Freshly picked capers – an island staple – are being pickled in a dish on a corner of the table.*

LEFT: *By the terrace, a monumental prickly pear tree grows out of a rock. The special utensil that sits on the ledge is used to pick the exotic fruit.*

SOLITARY LIVING

Near the village of Kallitsos on Sériphos stands the Greek Orthodox monastery of Taxiarchon, which dates from the 15th century. The monastery is made up of monks' cells set into the thick enclosing wall, a library with Byzantine manuscripts, and an 18th-century church with images of the famous archangels Gabriel and Michael, protectors of the island. Today, only one monk lives there, in magnificent solitude.

ABOVE: *Bell towers rise up in the center of the monastery's complex of buildings.*

LEFT: *The tiny windows of the monks' cells punctuate the thick walls of the monastery.*

ABOVE: *The white monastery is set in an arid landscape at the top of a hill overlooking the sea.*

LEFT: *The chapel is at the center of the interior courtyard. The entire building, inside and out, is freshly painted by its only inhabitant every spring.*

ABOVE AND RIGHT: Makarios, the monk who still lives in the monastery, stands in the main room. On the wall hang portraits of his spiritual ancestors, who inhabited the monastery in the past.

LEFT: One of the empty monks' cells has been converted into a larder. Goat's-milk cheeses made by Makarios age on ceiling-hung bamboo racks.

THE SUMMER HOUSE

For thousands of years travelers have appreciated the qualities that

The cult of simplicity and authenticity is growing. New values are establishing themselves. Many people who might formerly have chosen the frantic social life and luxurious amenities of tourist resorts are seeking out a simpler, more relaxed, and primitive life-style. Owning a small house on a remote island is now seen as the ultimate luxury.

Drawn by the climate and natural resources and seduced by the charm of the

make Greece a summer paradise. Now foreign visitors as well as

vernacular architecture, vacationers are choosing what were once fishermen's modest abodes or ship-captains' aristocratic residences for a new kind of vacation living.

OPPOSITE: A tourist map, airmail envelopes, postcards, vacation snap shots, seashells, and sunglasses create an enticing informal still life in a summer

vacationing Greeks want to become integrated in the local life.

bedroom of a vacation house on the island of Sériphos.

THIS PAGE: Ideal abodes for summer include a tent on a beach or a grottolike home on a rock surrounded by the sea.

AMONG FRIENDS

Solitude and an opportunity for friends to be together were two goals in the renovation of a complex of three tiny houses on the island of Sériphos. The structures were mostly in ruins, reduced to a pile of stones; the owners – a French journalist, along with a French architect and his wife – completely rebuilt them in the unpretentious spirit of the islands.

Each of the buildings, inside and out, has been designed to provide simple but perfectly appointed places in which to enjoy in the summer all the things that one yearns for during the rest of the year – sun, rest, and conviviality.

ABOVE: *Once in a while a donkey crosses the path between two of the buildings.*

LEFT: *The third house in the complex is a tiny guest suite.*

ABOVE: *The main house with its three levels is at the crossing of two village paths.*

LEFT: *Because the main house is set on a hill, its terrace commands a wide view of the sea and sky.*

ABOVE AND ABOVE RIGHT: An eclectic collection of blue glass objects is arranged in symmetrical still lifes on two windowsills.

LEFT: The living space in the main house includes an open kitchen and sitting area. A door leads to the courtyard.

BELOW LEFT: The large piece of slate that functions as a kitchen counter rests on four rocks above the stair.

RIGHT: *Situated at the top of the main house, the pale blue and white bedroom takes advantage of a magnificent view and is open to the elements.*

BELOW RIGHT: *Another bedroom set in the rock has a grottolike feeling. Small windows and thick walls keep the room cool.*

BELOW: *Two mattresses – for single or double occupancy – are set in a corner of the mezzanine bedroom.*

ABOVE: *A selection of summer reading sits on a windowsill on the mezzanine.*

LEFT AND BELOW: *The guest house has been built into the rock. A banquette-lined seating area, a small eating area, and a tiny open kitchen – all made of stone – are included on the ground floor.*

LEFT: *On one of the kitchen counters, an enamel coffee pot has been filled with the vibrantly colored geraniums that grow wild on the island.*

RIGHT: *The third house in the complex also features a mezzanine bedroom. Instead of stone, wood has been used as the building material.*

BELOW RIGHT: *With its wall built against the rock, the living area is austere. The folding canvas chairs are often carried out to the courtyard.*

BELOW FAR RIGHT: *One of the walls of the small bathroom is of natural rock.*

203

SHIP-CAPTAIN'S HOUSE

On the tourist-filled island of Rhodes, in the Dodecanese, the village of Líndos is the most exclusive resort in which to spend the summer. Ship-captains' houses that date from the early 18th century have become chic residences for the international jet set.

The house, once lived in by the archeologist who discovered the acropolis of Lindos at the beginning of the 20th century is, typically for the village, located directly on the street. The front door is set within a porch, and the courtyard is paved with pebbles called *krokalia.* Local textiles, a few pieces of pottery, and simple rustic furniture are among the unpretentious furnishings.

ABOVE: *The second-floor terrace is paved with the traditional black-and-white pebbles of the island of Rhodes.*

LEFT: *An exterior stair links the courtyard to a bedroom.*

LEFT: Small windows punctuate the wall of the bedroom floor.

LEFT: On the lower terrace, a white-painted sofa has been covered with blue cushions.

LEFT: The decorative motif in plaster seems to match the lace-edged pillowcase.

RIGHT AND FAR RIGHT: Both inside and outside, the floors of the house have been paved with pebbles laid in a decorative, fanciful pattern.

CENTER RIGHT: A craftsman on Rhodes made the long table with its abstract design of a hibiscus blossom.

BELOW RIGHT: On the ground floor, the traditional sleeping platform is a convivial corner.

BELOW CENTER RIGHT: According to Turkish custom, the mattresses in the bedroom are on either side of the fireplace.

BELOW FAR RIGHT: Old tinted prints hang on an antique weaving and are lined up on the storage trunk.

ABOVE: *The roomy eat-in kitchen is open to the courtyard.*

LEFT: *A glass panel framed in wood functions as a shower curtain in the tiny bathroom.*

ABOVE: *One of the bedrooms is completely lined with windows covered by traditional Greek blue-and-white cotton curtains. A mattress sits directly on the raised platform. The two low tables are Turkish.*

RIGHT: *A collection of straw hats decorates the wall.*

PANORAMIC VIEW

Located on a steep rock nestled between two chapels, Yorgos Zaphiriou's house has what is probably the most spectacular view on the island of Sériphos. Zaphiriou, a civil engineer from Athens, had the house rebuilt by local craftsmen using traditional building techniques.

Inside, all the rooms were designed around the existing natural rocks and were focused to take advantage of the views.

ABOVE: One of the terraces looks out on an unobstructed vista of the port of Sériphos and the island of Siphnos that can be seen far in the distance.

LEFT: The main entrance to the house opens into the kitchen.

RIGHT: At dusk, the lighted house is framed by two chapels.

LEFT: *The stone building conforms to its rocky site.*

LEFT: *Huge pottery jars decorate one of the terraces. White canvas and wood deck chairs always face the view.*

RIGHT: Double banquettes fitted with cotton-covered pillows provide comfortable seating on either side of the fireplace.

RIGHT: One of the bedrooms is carved directly out of rock. The mattress covered in white cotton seems to blend in with the whitewashed stone.

ABOVE AND LEFT: *The small kitchen features a traditional plate rack, an old café table, a wooden chest topped with a banquette, and a shallow marble sink.*

RIGHT: Stones, pieces of pottery, and bits of iron picked up on island walks are set out on a wood chest.

FAR RIGHT: Under the window, the stone wall acts as a backrest for the banquette.

RIGHT: In the ground-floor bedroom, a table is draped with a Greek cotton cloth.

FAR RIGHT: A straw hat sits on an old-fashioned Greek chair by the terrace door in the second-floor master bedroom.

ART DIRECTION

A passion for boats is evident in Nikos Kostopoulos's two-room house on Sériphos. The art director has relied on a few small objects to transform a tiny, rudimentary dwelling into an imaginative, nearly abstract environment. Model boats, seashells, and plaster casts are part of a series of intriguing still-life compositions that reflect Kostopoulos's exuberant personality.

ABOVE: The houses that constitute the village seem to billow like a white sail on the hillside of Sériphos.

LEFT: A blue-painted niche acts as a box frame for a model boat and a small Cycladic chapel.

RIGHT: The facade has a haphazard arrangement of random-sized doors and windows.

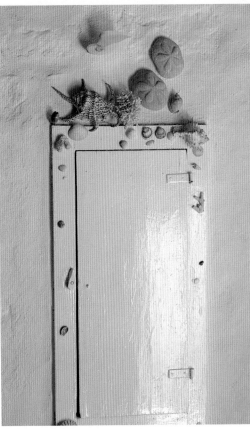

ABOVE FAR LEFT: *A pair of handcrafted baskets stand side by side under the window near the fireplace.*

ABOVE CENTER LEFT: *The old child's rowboat is suspended above an antique commode.*

FAR LEFT AND LEFT: *White lace curtains edge the sink and shelves in the minuscule kitchen.*

CENTER LEFT: *Seashells are artistically strewn around the built-in cupboard.*

ABOVE LEFT AND ABOVE: *An armada of model boats sails across the living room walls.*

INTERNATIONAL STYLE

The village house on Pátmos in the Dodecanese, like many others on this volcanic island, was bought in the last two decades by members of the international intelligentsia.

Now completely restored and furnished in a traditional style, the large stone house is where a family is reunited in the summer.

ABOVE: At the monastery of Saint John the Divine, the terrace overlooks the sea.

LEFT: The exterior dining area is shaded with a roof of twigs. A stone banquette follows the oval shape of the room.

221

LEFT: *The doors framed in natural stone and the graceful stone arches are typical of Pátmos.*

BELOW LEFT: *The rugs in the traditionally furnished living room were woven on the island.*

RIGHT: *The stair leads from the terrace to the front hall.*

CENTER RIGHT: *A period mirror framed in gilt hangs in the living room.*

FAR RIGHT: *At the top of the landing, a tray for serving coffee sits on a Turkish table.*

BELOW RIGHT: *One of the important pieces of furniture in the living room is a 19th-century antique Greek secretary.*

BELOW CENTER RIGHT: *A traditional painted tin tray holds two antique pewter pitchers.*

BELOW FAR RIGHT: *A paisley throw covers a round side table.*

223

ABOVE: *On the desk, vintage family photographs are assembled in an antique frame.*

TOP LEFT, TOP RIGHT, AND RIGHT: *The second-floor bedroom area is imaginatively separated from the study with a series of recycled wood screens that date from the time of the Turkish occupation.*

PIGEON HOUSE

On the rocky hillside far above the hubbub of the fashionable resort of Mykonos stands a tiny retreat that was once only a pigeon house.

If, for certain people, vacations are synonymous with companionship and entertaining, others prefer solitude and a return to nature. There is no electricity or running water, and only a few recycled objects and pieces of furniture are used in the minimal interior.

ABOVE: The retreat is made up of three elements – the original birdhouse, a cube-shaped living area and kitchen, and a small square bedroom.

LEFT: With its crown of whitewashed slate shards, the pigeon house is a form of vernacular architecture.

ABOVE: Slate steps lead up to the living area above the kitchen. Water is drawn from a wall-hung tin fountain near the kitchen door.

LEFT: The small courtyard is paved in slate. A large flat stone functions as a low table. Simple rush stools provide seating.

ABOVE FAR LEFT: The curtain in the living area is made of cotton. Lighting is provided by an oil lamp and candles.

ABOVE CENTER LEFT: A fabric remnant, an arrangement of wildflowers, and a bouquet of dried herbs tied to an old hat rack are minimal yet poetic details of the white interior.

ABOVE LEFT AND CENTER LEFT: Glass-filled open niches let daylight into the house.

ABOVE: In the sparse living area, a plaster relief recalls Mykonos's famous chapels.

FAR LEFT: A piece of old decorative ironwork echoes the semi-circular shape of the fireplace.

LEFT: Geraniums are framed by one of the wall openings.

DECORATIVE ORNAMENT

The impressive ship-captain's house on Líndos dominates the water like a medieval fortress. The stone building is of oriental influence and is decorated with carved motifs that hint at its highly respectable origins.

The house is large enough to accommodate many people but can also function as a private domain that is insulated from the crowds descending on the island resort in summer.

ABOVE: *The house is set on a hill dominating the bay.*

LEFT: *Comfortable lounge chairs on the back terrace are set out for sunbathing.*

ABOVE: *A bougainvillea grows in a broken whitewashed jar, which is held together with metal wire.*

LEFT: *The main courtyard has a characteristic* krokalia *pebble floor that has been laid in a symbolic geometric pattern.*

ABOVE: *An arched doorway leads from the courtyard to a small adjacent street.*

ABOVE RIGHT AND RIGHT: *During the summer, meals can be taken in the open-air dining room under the shade of a fig tree. The date the house was restored is written out in the traditional manner with pebbles on the ground.*

ABOVE: *A guest bedroom has the platform, fireplace, and double banquettes that typify the Turkish style on Líndos.*

ABOVE LEFT: *Steep steps lead to a small rear garden.*

LEFT: *Rustic kitchen utensils sit on the slate counter.*

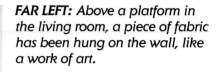

FAR LEFT: *Above a platform in the living room, a piece of fabric has been hung on the wall, like a work of art.*

LEFT: *In the bedroom, one of the stone walls has been left bare.*

BELOW FAR LEFT AND BELOW LEFT: *The large living room, called a sala, is typical of houses in the Dodecanese. It is divided into two areas that are connected with a vaulted arch. The painted ceiling and stained-glass window are oriental.*

RIGHT: A mattress and pillows top a storage chest in the living room. The textile wall hanging was crafted in the Dodecanese.

LEFT: *The raised platform at the end of the living room was traditionally used for sleeping.*

BELOW LEFT AND RIGHT: *The master bedroom is on the second floor and has been furnished with an antique Greek bed in iron and cut-out tin. The design of the pebble border echoes the graceful shape of the bed frame.*

OUTDOOR LIVING

Like many of the smaller houses in Líndos, on the island of Rhodes, the vacation home is centered around an outdoor courtyard that has been lushly planted. Local craftsmen made the furniture, which dates from the sixties and seventies. Relaxed and comfortable, the house is meant for the enjoyment of easy summer living.

ABOVE: *The courtyard with its floor of pebbles functions as an outdoor living room. The chairs are handcrafted in fifties style.*

LEFT: *A neoclassical facade marks the entrance to the house.*

ABOVE: *A window, set into thick stone walls, offers a view of the Líndos countryside.*

LEFT: *A marble tabletop set on the pebble floor creates a play of rich textures.*

240

RIGHT: The bathroom has been completely renovated. The highly polished marble floor and sink contrast with the rustic beamed ceiling.

241

COUNTRY PLEASURE

Once a simple farmhouse, the weekend and vacation home situated on a large property in the countryside near Athens, has now been renovated and enlarged. Generously proportioned terraces provide open-air spaces for living and dining and are pleasing additions to a modern house that retains its rustic charm.

ABOVE: The Roman-tiled roof provides a shaded place to sit on a hot summer afternoon.

LEFT: An overgrown stone path leads to the entrance.

LEFT: *A thick forest of trees creates an oasis of privacy by the swimming pool.*

LEFT: *The house is focused around a paved terrace.*

243

ABOVE FAR LEFT: *The entrance hall has rough stone walls, a metal-studded door, and a floor of patinated terra-cotta tile.*

ABOVE CENTER LEFT: *The low table on the terrace was made from an old metal-studded door.*

ABOVE LEFT: *An antique wood-and-metal door has recently been repainted by a contemporary folk artist.*

FAR LEFT: *The wall facing the main terrace calls to mind a romantic ruin that is being overgrown by vegetation.*

ABOVE: *The long refectory table in the dining room has been set for lunch.*

CENTER LEFT: *The painting of a factory and a few branches in an antique pitcher create a still life full of atmosphere.*

LEFT: *Rustic pottery is displayed on the thick wood shelves in the dining room.*

EASY LIVING

The vacation house in the village of Pátmos, on the island of the same name, was renovated for a foreign couple by Michel Photiadis and is as fresh-looking as it is refined. By adding a luxurious bathroom, a large master bedroom, and a number of loggias, the architect has created an elegant but easy-to-live-in summer home.

ABOVE: *The interior courtyard is completely enclosed and separated from the street.*

LEFT: *The flat terra-cotta roofs of neighboring houses can be seen from the terrace.*

ABOVE: *Oil lamps stand on a chest near the front door.*

LEFT: *A stone doorway frames a view of the bedroom suite.*

TOP: *A naive painting hangs by the glossy-painted double doors.*

ABOVE: *Country-style chairs are juxtaposed with a period mirror and a wood chest.*

RIGHT: *The bedroom suite is made up of a ground-floor sitting room and a sleeping loggia over the bathroom.*

TOP: *At the end of the living room, a pair of symmetrical doorways opens onto the dining room.*

ABOVE: *Wide steps descend to the basement of the house.*

LEFT: *Antique pots are arranged on the small gallery over the stairs.*

ABOVE: The large bathroom has been outfitted with a freestanding tub as well as an electric towel-warmer.

ABOVE: Flat terra-cotta bricks, once used for roofs on Pátmos, are now laid on the floor.

RIGHT: The kitchen is off the courtyard.

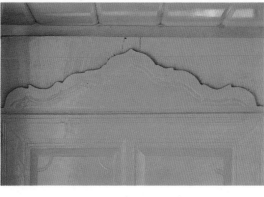

ABOVE: *The Greek half-canopied iron beds are draped in white cotton.*

ABOVE: *A piece of carved wood molding adorns the bathroom door.*

LEFT: *Ornate interior shutters are one of the elements of an affluent house.*

251

SIXTIES STYLE

Built during the 1960s in the Attica region near Athens, the contemporary house in Pórto Ráfti is used as a summer home by wealthy and knowledgeable collectors of modern art. The owners have integrated paintings and sculptures by the best-known contemporary Greek artists into the house and its verandas, and large garden.

From its dramatic red front door to its custom-designed furnishings, the tasteful residence is a perfect example of a sixties style that is being re-appreciated today.

ABOVE: *Once merely utilitarian, the enormous whitewashed oil jars are now considered fine art.*

LEFT: *The long, low, one-story house is typical of the sixties.*

LEFT: *A sculpture of a nude by Memos Makris stands in the garden that descends to the sea.*

LEFT: *The naturalistic pool is connected to the house by a stone terrace.*

ABOVE: *A red metal-studded door marks the entrance.*

ABOVE: *On the terrace near the pool, a metal sculpture by Alex Mylona is displayed by a wall.*

RIGHT: *A steep path leads down to a private cove.*

ABOVE: *In the large living room, a corner has been set aside for playing cards. The bridge table and chairs were custom-designed for the room by T.H. Gibbings, the American furniture designer. The painting is by Theodoros Stamos.*

ABOVE RIGHT: *A mosaic by Zizi Makris is above the wicker sofa on the veranda.*

RIGHT: *The all-white dining room is focused around an enormous colorful tapestry by Yannis Faïtakis.*

ABOVE: *A collection of minerals is displayed above the modern mantelpiece.*

ABOVE LEFT: *A pair of openings separates the spacious hall from the dining room.*

LEFT: *The pattern in the living room carpet woven by Yannis Faïtakis depicts minerals that mirror the examples displayed on the bookcases. The pillows are needlepoint seashell-shaped.*

GUEST HOUSE

When Vassilis Tseghis, an Athenian interior decorator, bought his house on Sériphos, it was in ruins. Situated in Hóra, the highest village on the arid and rocky island, the building was completely reconstructed and furnished as a summer residence for the designer and the many friends he likes to entertain there.

Outdoor staircases connect the numerous outbuildings that have been turned into guest rooms. Although the exterior is based on the popular traditional house type, the interior has been completely adapted to vacation life.

ABOVE: The large house is made of a series of structures connected by stairs and terraces.

LEFT: Double stable doors open into a small hall.

LEFT AND BELOW LEFT: The roof terraces have a panoramic view of the arid landscape and the sea beyond.

TOP: *A new interior stone stair, which matches the staircases of the exterior, leads to the mezzanine bedroom.*

ABOVE: *Because the spaces in the house were restructured, one of the fireplaces has ended up in the entrance hall.*

LEFT: *The front door and the slate threshold have been framed in blue.*

TOP: *A traditional island bench provides extra seating.*

ABOVE: *Silver accessories are set out in the living room.*

RIGHT: *The extravagantly pillow-ed banquette in the living room can be glimpsed through the rough-hewn doorway.*

FAR LEFT: The double banquette with pink pillows, the graphically woven floor covering, and the ancient stones are sophisticated additions to the interior.

LEFT: An old-fashioned gilt mirror reflects the bedroom.

BELOW FAR LEFT: The tiny kitchen serves the needs of the occupants of the guest room.

BELOW CENTER LEFT: A steep narrow stair with slate treads leads to a roof terrace.

BELOW LEFT: In one of the guest studios, a dressing table is perched on the mezzanine.

RIGHT: The iron four-poster bed is draped in the soft white woven cotton that can be found on the islands.

SAFE HAVEN

Although small in scale, the house in the village of Líndos has all the characteristics of the more prepossessing homes of ship captains. The richly carved stone facade is hidden at the end of an interior courtyard, as befits a building that was originally meant as a safe haven. Now transformed into a summer retreat for an Italian family, the house, with its enclosed courtyard, is a buffer against more modern foes, which include the hordes of tourists invading Líndos during the summer.

ABOVE: *The sailboat depicted in* krokalia *refers to the seafaring origins of the house.*

LEFT: *A carved-stone rope motif delineates the entrance arch.*

ABOVE: *The roof-terrace floor is also paved with pebbles.*

LEFT: *At the end of the hidden courtyard oriental motifs are mixed with early Christian symbols on the carved stone facade.*

265

TOP: *Hibiscus and geraniums grow in pots in the courtyard.*

ABOVE: *A still life of driftwood and broken pottery has been composed against a wall.*

TOP AND RIGHT: *A deep arch shelters the summer dining area.*

ABOVE: *The facade of one of the bedrooms has a distinctly medieval look.*

RIGHT AND BELOW FAR RIGHT:
Two platforms provide sleeping
areas at one end of the sala.

BELOW RIGHT: The corner cupboard is a space-saving solution.

269

BOLD COLOR

The house that belongs to Michel Photiadis, an Athenian architect, and his wife, Melpo, is at the foot of the legendary monastery of Saint John the Divine on Pátmos. The building is made up of three separate pristine white structures – two comprising the main house, the third reserved for guests.

Inside, the architect's choice of colors is as bold as it is surprising. Instead of using the traditional pale blue, he has painted the woodwork in the unusual colors of dark green and bright orange.

ABOVE: *The geometric outline of the roofs of the Photiadis house can be clearly seen from the monastery.*

LEFT: *One of the alleyways of the village runs underneath the guest house.*

ABOVE: *A roof shields the ceramic-tile table and canvas chairs in the courtyard.*

LEFT: *The guest house has a central courtyard that connects two of the bedrooms.*

ABOVE: A bouquet of bay leaves decorates a painted tin spoon-holder.

LEFT: The oversized pots and antique lamp are in the terracotta brick-floored entrance hall.

ABOVE RIGHT AND ABOVE FAR RIGHT: The small sitting room is furnished with antique bentwood pieces. The perforated engravings on the screen are lit from behind.

RIGHT AND FAR RIGHT: Hurricane lamps stand on the massive antique desk in one of the reception rooms. The woodwork is painted dark green.

RIGHT AND FAR RIGHT: The bedrooms are minimally furnished with cotton bedcovers and mattresses set into carved wood box frames.

273

LEFT: *The wood trim, doors, and shutters in the guest room have been painted in bright orange.*

BELOW FAR LEFT: *Terra-cotta tiles line the counter and floor of the renovated bathroom.*

BELOW LEFT: *Four antique chairs are lined up against the whitewashed wall.*

RIGHT: A pair of rickety antique iron beds, woven purple bed-spreads, and orange shutters contribute to the naive charm of the room.

275

HOUSE AND GARDEN

One of the benefits of having a vacation house a little outside the village of Hóra on Pátmos is being able to take advantage of the pleasures of the garden as well as the sea. Roses and geraniums bloom in profusion at the edge of the wide terraces, where a sweeping view of the sea and the neighboring islands can be enjoyed.

The stone house is furnished with rustic Greek pieces. But the bedrooms in particular, and their antique Greek beds, draped with American quilts, are the essence of charm.

ABOVE: *The white house can be seen from the road that goes up to the village.*

LEFT: *An extravagant geranium plant grows on the terrace.*

LEFT: *Potted geraniums parade up the steps that lead to the roof.*

277

ABOVE: The large bathroom has a floor of brick terra-cotta tiles.

ABOVE FAR LEFT: The wide banquettes are fitted with wool-covered mattresses.

ABOVE LEFT: A comfortable low sofa, usually located inside, has been brought out to the terrace.

FAR LEFT AND LEFT: Flowering plants frame the wide stone terrace off the living room.

BELOW FAR LEFT: The covered veranda with its comfortable pillowed sofa provides a shady place to sit outdoors.

BELOW LEFT: On the second floor, an open walkway links the bedrooms to the bathroom.

ABOVE RIGHT AND RIGHT: The wood-beam-ceilinged living room is comfortably furnished. Colorful woven rugs cover the wide-plank floor. The glass hurricane lanterns are used on windy days.

TOP AND LEFT: *An antique Greek canopy bed is the focus of the bedroom. The new lattice-fronted closets were designed to coordinate with the original corner cupboards, which are of Turkish inspiration.*

ABOVE: *An American quilt covers the bed in the all-blue-and-white guest room.*

FAIRY TALE

The house on the island of Rhodes looks as if it came out of a fairy tale. Set behind thick walls, it is a feminine and intensely personal retreat built around a hidden garden.

Mattresses placed on the floor, pillows covered with old linens, and a few basic pieces of furniture contribute to the bohemian feeling of the summer home.

ABOVE: *The enclosed courtyard is centered around an old tree.*

LEFT: *A set of bricklayer's tools recalls the persistence of the craft tradition on the island.*

ABOVE: Pillows and mattresses are laid out on the terrace.

LEFT: Because it is left outside, the frame of the island bench has a weathered look.

LEFT: *A rug and mattresses cover the pebble floor in the informal living room. Three low Turkish café tables double as trays.*

RIGHT: *The lace pillowcases on the banquette were made by women in the island villages.*

FAR RIGHT: *An antique textile hangs over an etched storage chest in the living room.*

BELOW RIGHT: *The date of one of the house's restorations is inscribed in pebbles inside the front door.*

BELOW FAR RIGHT: *A dish storage rack hangs above the terrazzo sink counter.*

ABOVE: *In the bathroom, a mirror stands in what was once the bread oven.*

RIGHT: *All the woodwork in the master bedroom has been painted a brilliant blue.*

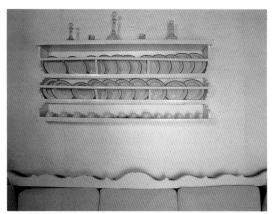

TOP: *The everyday dishes are kept close at hand in a dish rack in the kitchen.*

ABOVE: *Over the bed hangs a needlepoint picture embroidered by a local woman.*

ABOVE LEFT: *A step has been built into the storage chests for access to the staircase to the mezzanine.*

LEFT: *Roses from the garden echo the embroidered designs of the tablecloth.*

LEFT: *A private swimming pool in the center of Athens with a view on the Acropolis adds to the pleasure of living in a city where summer lasts most of the year, and temperatures often climb to over 100° Fahrenheit.*

GREEK LEXICON

Illustrations by Liz Gibbons

One of the pleasures of appreciating a foreign land is to discover and learn about the particular traditions of the country – music, art, architecture, and food.

ARTS AND ENTERTAINMENT

BOUZOUKI
Pear-shaped stringed instrument, related to the mandolin, on which popular Greek music is played. A smaller version of the instrument is called a *baglamas.*

GLYKOTHIKI
Brass or silver holder for spoons used to serve sweets.

KALAMATIANOS
The most traditional dance in which men and women form a circle and perform intricate steps. Other popular dances are the *zeymbekiko,* a dance for men only; the *tsifteteli,* its female version; the *tsamikos,* an acrobatic dance for men; the *hassapiko,* known as the butcher's dance; and the *syrtaki,* a simplified version of the *hassapiko.*

KENDIMA
Typical Greek embroidery with motifs inspired by flowers, animals, landscapes, and seascapes, as well as other elements of the natural world and mythology. All over Greece, embroidery is women's work. Young girls, who have the time and inclination for the craft, prepare their dowries sewing *kendimata* with intricate and colorful designs on the family linens.

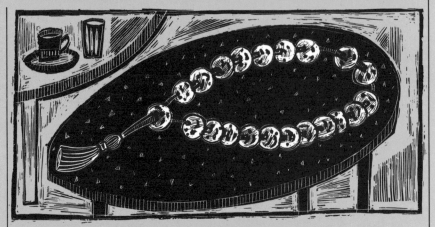

KERAMIKA
Ceramic plates and bowls decorated with colorful designs. The center for the craft is Rhodes and its neighboring islands. *Keramika* are proudly displayed in cupboards or hung on the walls of rooms.

KOMBOLOÏ
Worry beads that men hold and run their fingers over all day long. *Komboloï,* originated in the Middle East but have no religious significance.

TAVAS

The brass or galvanized metal tray used in traditional Greek cafés and *tavernas* for serving ouzo and coffee with the accompanying glass of water.

TAVLI

Backgammon. *Tavli*, played on boards with inlaid stone or wood, is a national pastime.

ARCHITECTURE AND DESIGN

AKROKERAMA AND KOLONAKI

Terra-cotta elements that adorn the rooflines of neoclassical houses.

ANEMOMILI

Windmills. Set on hills to take advantage of the winds, *anemomili* still dot many of the islands. Most are now purely decorative but once were used to grind wheat.

BALCONI

A balcony with a railing of stone, wood, or cast iron, that is often found on the exterior of town houses.

CAMINADA

Traditional chimney. Shapes and materials vary with the islands. Whether of terra-cotta or stone, each *caminada* has its distinct design.

FLITZANAKI

Small, heavy china cup with a solid handle in which Greek coffee is traditionally served.

FLOKATI

Carpet made from undyed, long-haired lamb's wool.

ICONOSTASI

The small cupboard used to store religious objects, such as icons and oil lamps.

KALIMERA

The Greek word for good morning, usually written on a small mirror that hangs inside the front entrance of many popular houses.

KILIM

A two-sided flat woven carpet. *Kilim* is a Turkish word adopted throughout the Orient to describe this kind of carpet.

KOURELOU

Striped, woven rag rug traditionally used to cover floors and walls.

KREVATI

Cast-iron bed, often decorated with floral motifs.

KROUNOS

A small fountain made of galvanized metal that is hung on the wall and sometimes painted. The *krounos* is common in popular houses without running water.

MANGALI

Charcoal-burning brass brazier, of oriental inspiration, that is found in the north of Greece and used for heating.

KROKALIA

Decorative mosaic of pebbles, used traditionally in the gardens and courtyards of the islands of the Dodecanese.

MEANDROS
Decorative border motif that has been predominant since antiquity. Symbolizing the continuation of life, *meandros* still appears in contemporary buildings.

MOUSSANDRA
Particularly common in northern Greece, a large chest often carved and decoratively painted in which the family linens are stored.

NISSIOTIKO
Decorative wood bench crafted on the islands. The version used in churches and monasteries is called *papadistiko.*

PERISTEREONAS
Pigeonhouse. Openings in the shape of stars, circles, and diamonds punctuate these limestone structures. The *peristereonas* can be 20 feet high and house 500 birds.

PIATOTHIKI
Wall-hung rack or cupboard in which the everyday ceramic dishes are stored.

PITHARI
Large terra-cotta containers, some of which are glazed, for olive oil or grain.

ROPTRO
Most doors are adorned with a brass knocker or *roptro.* A hand holding a ball is a typical design.

SPERVERI
Embroidered curtains that are attached to the ceiling and form a cone-shaped enclosure for the bed.

TAVANI
Ceiling. A major design element in the house. In the popular house it is of natural cane, wood, or slate. In more bourgeois houses, the *tavani* is carved or painted.

DELICACIES

AVGOLEMONO
A combination of eggs and lemon used for thickening soups and sauces.

BAKLAVA
Sweet pastry consisting of thin pastry dough (phyllo) layered with nuts soaked in syrup and honey.

CAPARI
Capers. The bud of a flower that grows on stone walls in arid regions. Pickled *capari* are used as a condiment.

DOLMADES
Vine leaves stuffed with meat and rice.

ELIES
The olive, harvested in January and February, is the most important crop in Greece. There are at least ten different kinds from the dark brown *kalamata*, grown in the south of the Peloponnese, to the large lighter-skinned variety that comes from the area around Delphi.

ELLINIKOS KAFES
Greek coffee, also called Turkish coffee, drunk at all hours of the day and night. Served in small cups, it is ordered *glyko* (sweet), *metrio* (medium sweet), or *sketo* (without sugar). Once the coffee is served, it is never stirred. The grounds are left at the bottom of the cup to be read by fortune tellers.

FETA
White salted cheese made from goat or ewe milk, which is eaten sliced or crumbled into salads.

SYKA
Dried figs that are eaten in the winter, often accompanied with ouzo.

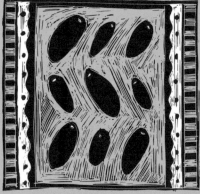

KOULOURI
White bread shaped in a ring, covered with sesame seeds.

KOURABIEDES
Crescent-shaped cookies, covered in powdered sugar, that are traditional at Christmastime.

LADI
Olive oil. An essential ingredient of Greek food. The best quality *ladi* comes from the Peloponnese area, particularly the towns of Kalamata and Messinia and the islands of Sifnos and Mytilene.

MEZEDAKIA
Snacks served in cafés and *tavernas* with ouzo or wine. A typical assortment includes *tzatziki* (a yogurt, cucumber, and garlic dip), *taramosalata* (fish-roe pâté), *dolmades* (vine leaves stuffed with meat and rice), *kalamarakia* (fried squid), and *tyropitakia* (cheese wrapped in phyllo dough).

MOUSSAKAS
Traditional Greek dish made of layers of eggplant, sliced potatoes, and minced meat with a béchamel sauce.

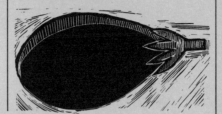

OUZO
The traditional aperitif of Greece, made by distilling the residue of pressed grapes that have been flavored with aromatic seeds and herbs, especially anise. The addition of a few drops of water gives the clear liquid its milky color.

RETSINA
The national white wine of Greece. Its name comes from the pine tree resin that is added after fermentation as a preservative.

RODI
The pomegranate – a symbol of fertility and prosperity. On New Year's Day, a pomegranate is crushed on the floor of the house and its scattered seeds signify good fortune for the rest of the year.

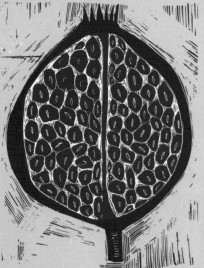

SOUVLAKI
Pork or veal cooked on skewers and served in pita bread with tomatoes and onions or yogurt flavored with garlic.

VASILIKOS
Basil. A common herb that is rarely used in cooking but grows in pots in front of nearly every house.

YAOURTI
Greek yogurt, thick in texture, is often eaten with honey.

CALENDAR EVENTS

SAINT BASIL, NEW YEAR'S DAY
Saint Basil is Greece's Santa Claus, and gifts are exchanged on this day rather than on Christmas. At midnight the *vassilopita*, or Saint Basil's cake, is served. The person who finds the hidden coin in the *vassilopita* can look forward to a year of good luck.

EPIPHANY, JANUARY 6
The blessing of the waters. A religious custom that includes a priest's throwing a cross in the water. Young people then retrieve the cross and return it to the church.

APOKRIES
Three weeks before Lent. Masked and costumed revelers dance in the streets during carnival, just before Lent.

INDEPENDENCE DAY, MARCH 25
The army parades in many towns on this day, to celebrate the anniversary of the War of Independence of 1821.

GOOD FRIDAY
Colorful religious processions with representations of the body of Christ covered with flowers take place in the streets of most towns and villages.

EASTER

The Greek Orthodox Easter, which is not at the same time as the Roman Catholic Easter, marks the Resurrection of Christ and is the most important religious event of the year. Real and artificial eggs, dyed red to signify the blood of Christ, decorate the shops and houses.

KINISSI, OR THE ASSUMPTION OF MARY, AUGUST 15

On this holiday, a pilgrimage, especially on the island of Tinos, pays homage to the Virgin Mary. In the Greek Orthodox religion, this holiday is celebrated in all the churches that carry the name of Mary.

CHRISTMAS, DECEMBER 25

On Christmas, a less important celebration than Easter, traditional foods such as *kourabiedes*, butter and sugar cookies, and *Christopsomo*, bread decorated with a cross, are served.

PROTOMAYA, MAY 1

A holiday and feast of the flowers. Wreaths are hung above doors and on balconies for good luck and to ward off the evil eye.

INDEX

STYLE LIBRARY

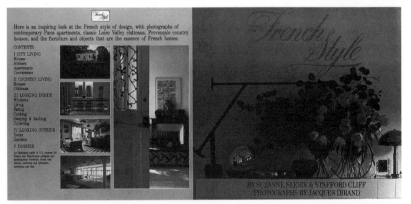

FRENCH STYLE
Suzanne Slesin and Stafford Cliff/Photographs by Jacques Dirand

"Not only an important contribution to the literature of interior decorating, but also a touchstone for our times." – Los Angeles Herald Examiner

For centuries the French have been celebrated for their *art de vivre*, and *French Style* is a book that captures the charm, vitality, and elegance of the contemporary French life-style as it is reflected in that country's interiors. Town and country houses, flats, lofts, ateliers, and chateaus demonstrate the range of French design tastes and provide many translatable decorating ideas. *French Style* exudes that special quality, a rare blend of magic, elegance, and sophistication for which the French are famous.

The directory provides a listing of sources for French and French-style antiques and contemporary furnishings.

ENGLISH STYLE
Suzanne Slesin and Stafford Cliff/Photographs by Ken Kirkwood

"A singularly beautiful and evocative look at the mix of formality, coziness, and comfort that is complex yet instantly recognizable as English Style." – Chicago Tribune

English Style richly illustrates the value of tradition and ingenuity in today's English interior design. From a grand manor house replete with chintzes to a London factory loft furnished with graphic severity, from a gabled country cottage to a Victorian terrace house with orginal William Morris wallpaper, each of these splendid interiors is quintessentially English.

More than 600 glorious full-color photographs accompany an informative text, and a catalogue of sources of English furnishings is included as well.

Like English literature and English manners, the English style of decorating has provided inspiration to generations of Americans and Europeans.

CARIBBEAN STYLE
Suzanne Slesin, Stafford Cliff, Jack Berthelot, Martine Gaumé, and Daniel Rozensztroch/Photographs by Gilles de Chabaneix

"A handsome book...that presents the Caribbean islands as a rich and distinctive aesthetic experience." – New York Times Book Review

A unique blend of travel book and design book, *Caribbean Style* offers a previously unseen view of the architecture, interior design, gardens, and life-style of Guadeloupe, Martinique, St. Barthélemy, Antigua, Nevis, Montserrat, Barbados, Haiti, and Jamaica. The book includes chapters on plantation houses, town houses, popular houses, contemporary houses, gardens, island vegetation and colors, climate and crops, and cultural heritage.

With this vivid portait of the Caribbean, you will almost feel the soft breezes, inhale the fragrance of tropical flowers, and luxuriate in the warmth of the sun.

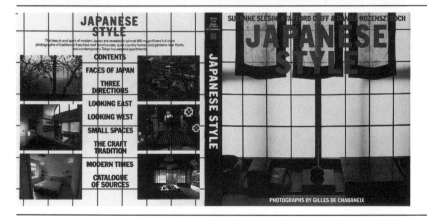

JAPANESE STYLE
Suzanne Slesin, Stafford Cliff, and Daniel Rozensztroch
Photographs by Gilles de Chabaneix

"A mesmerizing look at the rarefied and rarely visited Japanese home." – Vogue

A stylish, sophisticated, and often unexpected look at how the Japanese live today, as expressed through interior design, *Japanese Style* captures the richness and diversity of modern Japan. In almost 800 full-color photographs, the book presents a wide range of houses and apartments – from architect-designed contemporary homes to centuries-old farmhouses and inns. The locations include a fashion designer's luxurious Tokyo duplex, a stunning house and garden on a hillside near Kyoto, a traditional geisha house, and the country house of the renowned potter Shoji Hamada.

Japanese Style holds many lessons – and delights – for Westerners as it evokes the never-ending romance of Japan.

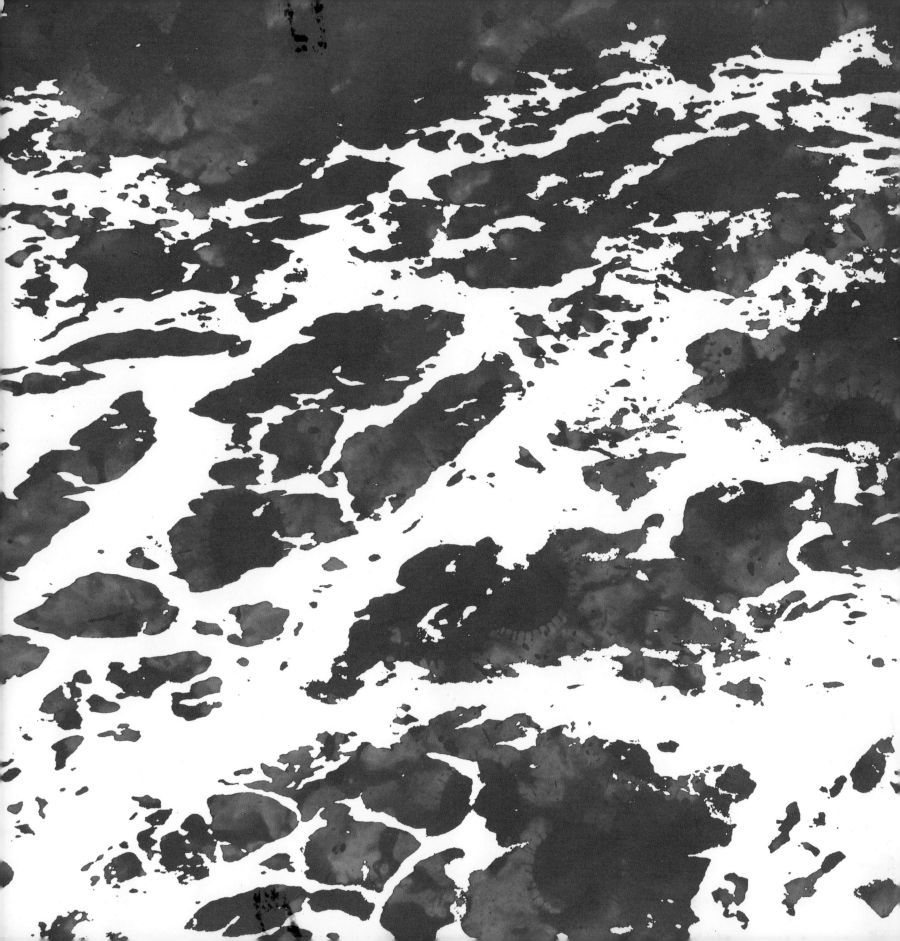